T0193520

MY
FIVE
MINUTE
BIBLE
STUDIES

27 ADVENTURES IN THE
OLD AND NEW TESTAMENTS

DON GORDON

WESTBOW
PRESS®
A DIVISION OF THOMAS NELSON
& ZONDERVAN

WestBow Press books may be ordered through booksellers or by contacting:

WestBow Press
A Division of Thomas Nelson & Zondervan
1663 Liberty Drive
Bloomington, IN 47403
www.westbowpress.com
844-714-3454

Scriptures taken from the Holy Bible, New International Version®, NIV®. Copyright © 1973, 1978, 1984, 2011 by Biblica, Inc.™ Used by permission of Zondervan. All rights reserved worldwide. www.zondervan.com The "NIV" and "New International Version" are trademarks registered in the United States Patent and Trademark Office by Biblica, Inc.®

ISBN: 978-1-6642-9527-8 (sc)
ISBN: 978-1-6642-9526-1 (hc)
ISBN: 978-1-6642-9528-5 (e)

Library of Congress Control Number: 2023904994

Print information available on the last page.

WestBow Press rev. date: 03/27/2023

This work in service to the Lord is dedicated to the loving memory of my dear wife, Zona Louise Lansche Gordon, whose beautiful life exemplified the best in faithful Christian walk.

CONTENTS

HOLY SCRIPTURE

The Bible is accepted generally by the Christian world as the inspired word of God and the text itself gives testimony to that truth (2Timothy 3:16).

There are reasons beyond simple conviction and faith to support that belief, and this treatment is an attempt toward that end. First a disclaimer: I assume no detailed knowledge of the history of development of the scripture, as an educated seminarian or well-versed Christian apologist would have; nevertheless, when we pick up that sacred book it is fair to consider how it came to be.

This is what we generally know. The Bible is made up of 66 books divided into two testaments written by 30 or more authors over a period spanning centuries. These men produced and copied multiple manuscripts that included at least three languages. Centuries later, other men compiled them into what we now know as the accepted canon, which then was translated into the other languages of the world, including English in 1611.

There are skeptics and agnostics who would argue that such a disparate and fragmented history militates against believing in the truth and validity of the scripture. A better conclusion is that the very process itself tends to confirm just the opposite.

Accordingly, one needs to consider the whole text of the Bible and ask oneself this question: How could an undertaking at the hands and minds of so many humans over vast periods of time produce the finished work we now see without divine guidance? In effect, we are speaking of a miracle.

In the Bible we find continuity, consistency, coherence. How else could teachings by Moses 4,000 years ago reach logical conclusion in the life and teaching of Jesus Christ as recorded by Matthew and others 2,000 years later? It was from a master plan conceived in eternity past that God erected His edifice, block by block, until we have the finished product that we now read, study, believe and seek to live by.

It is in the scripture that we discover the answers to the most profound questions of the human heart. How did we get here? What is life's purpose? What happens when we die? And will we live again? What is the source of evil? And is there redemption for our own part in it?

In some respects, it is as though a talented novelist were at work in the manuscripts, setting up scenarios in the Old Testament that would be fulfilled in the New, not necessarily in plain language, but seen through spiritual discernment by careful readers of the book. We see history repeating itself, as the Book of Ecclesiastes said it would. (1:9) Events in Genesis are relevant in Revelation. From Moses to the Apostle John.

The Old Testament includes uncommon wisdom, even for our day, things such as allowing land to remain fallow for a season, a lesson Americans learned the hard way only after the 1930s. Prophecies and their fulfillment abound. One cannot read the book of Isaiah and miss the prophecy of the coming Messiah. Psalm 22 describes details of the crucifixion in unmistakable terms.

Theologians use the term "types and shadows," referring to elements of the Old Testament that foreshadow the New. For instance, the healing of Naaman the leper in 2 Kings (5:14) was a picture of the salvation that Christ would bring. There are many other such examples, as well as multiple prophecies that tie the two testaments together and give credence to their inspiration.

The Bible is rich in symbolism, not always easy to understand. Readers often do not know whether to take a certain passage as literal or allegorical. Is hyperbole employed at times? Probably, but that also is part of its literary quality.

This book does not resemble a technical journal, a set of instructions, or a news story written with journalistic clarity. This may cause some even to doubt its validity, but a contrary view is this: The very fact of a book open to interpretation, to differing viewpoints in places, is a sign of the divine genius that brought it about.

Suppose the Bible's character were otherwise.. Where would discussion occur? What would stimulate the interest that the scripture engenders. Why would we need Sunday school, seminaries, and so forth? One or two readings of a so-called simple book would be sufficient for a lifetime. There would be no room for fresh revelation, growth in knowledge. Some say with accuracy that the scripture is pregnant. Why would we ask for one that is barren?

The Bible as it is leads to denominations. Fine. The human race is not so much in lockstep as to tastes, abilities, predispositions that we should all worship at identical churches in identical ways.

The diversity may lead to heresies, some would argue. True enough, but believers can deal with those. Think of the gospel as a river, with many eddies and currents. As long as it remains within its banks, meaning that the core doctrine of Christ is intact, Christians should be able to accept the differences. It is only when the floodwaters overflow the banks that false and dangerous doctrine occurs.

From the creation in Genesis 1:1 to the culmination of human events in Revelation 22 the scripture contains unity and purpose, the story of God's relationship with his people. How that story got from the mind of God into the hands of humanity can best be explained, not by the randomness of unrelated accidents, but by the divine intelligence of the Creator of the Universe.

WATER AND THE ROCK

T he two brothers, Moses, the lawgiver, and Aaron, the first in the Levitical priest line, dominated four early books of the Old Testament, two through five. But the discussion here will deal only with a single incident and its consequences.

The narrative is found in the 20th chapter of Numbers when the wandering Israelites thirsted for water, and the brothers were commissioned by God to respond to that need according to instructions. (20:8)

As a matter of background, the Israelite people after their deliverance from Egyptian slavery were led by Moses through the wilderness toward the Promised Land. It could be accurately stated that they complained a lot. They were critical of their leadership, demanded meat, lapsed at times into idolatry, expressed a wish to return to Egypt, and worst of all, out of unfounded fear and lack of faith, they refused to enter the land God had promised them.

Now at a place called Kadesh the general discontent over lack of water reached a high pitch. But God promised water. Moses and Aaron were ordered to speak to the rock and water would come forth. It must be noted that on a previous occasion, Moses as instructed had struck a rock with his staff and water was produced, so he had some experience with this sort of thing.

This time, however, his anger and impatience with his people apparently got the better of him, and after telling his charges what he thought about them and their constant complaining, he struck the rock with his staff--twice.

Moses and Aaron were both guilty of the sin of disobedience, one that a righteous God could not and would not overlook. Our first reaction might be to minimize the seriousness of the transgression. After all, Moses simply lost his temper for a moment, and with understandable cause. No, his act was far worse than that. He in effect had usurped God's glory and had taken it for himself. By his overt personal action, he had made it appear that he, not God, had supplied the water the people craved.

Incidentally, it is worth noting that despite the disobedience, water did pour forth. A gracious God did not withhold his blessing because of the failure of the leaders.

There would be a price to pay by the two brothers. We start with Aaron. His was a sin of omission. He had failed to speak as commanded, and judgment came quickly. First, he learned he would not live to see the promised land, but there was more. Moses was instructed to take Aaron and his son Eleazar upon a mountain where Moses would strip Aaron's garments and place them on the son. This amounted to a defrocking of Aaron from his position as the pre-eminent priest, much as a disgraced clergyman today might endure his removal. So not only would Aaron die, perhaps prematurely, but as a discredited priest. (Numbers 20:25-29)

This may seem harsh. But we have to remember Aaron's past, such as his leading role in the golden calf idolatry, and the way he from jealousy came against his brother over Moses' wife. He seemed to get a pass for those indiscretions, but maybe accountability came to him all at once.

Moses' judgment would come later. His sin was more egregious than Aaron's. It was a matter of both omission and commission, failing to speak and striking the rock. God would tell Moses that because of his actions at Kadesh, he like his brother would not enter the Promised Land, but in his case he would look on it from a distance. This may have been the greater punishment, allowing Moses to see what he could not have. (Deuteronomy 34: 1) For Moses, the experience likely led to a profound moment of regret about "what might have been." As he gazed across the Jordan to see the beauty of the Promised Land, he must have thought how much different the culminating years of his life would have been had he made a better choice. How many of us can fail to identify with that?

Moses uttered a plea to God to rescind the penalty, to no avail. He also reminded the people more than once that it was because of them that God has become angry with him.

There was some truth in that, but Moses, in common with all of us, should not have blamed others for his own mistake.

One of many lessons we can draw from the sin at the waters of Kadesh and its aftermath is God's demonstration that he truly is not a respecter of persons. All of the godly service Aaron and particularly Moses had performed in their remarkable lives did not immunize them from accountability for their transgressions. They were not allowed to built up credits against the day they would need them to offset their sin. Neither are we. God does not grade on some kind of balance sheet.

And we must know this: The judgment against Moses and Aaron was temporal, not eternal, which should be a comfort to all Christians who inevitably fail at times. We can be assured that the two brothers of the Bible are secure in the embrace of their Lord, in the same way all believes are or will be.

THE FIRST KING

The life story of Saul, Judah's first king, leaves many questions, few answers and some speculation, but the process of discovery can be intriguing.

The book of 2 Samuel carries the narrative. We see that the Israelites, during the time of the judges, decided they wanted a king as the other nations had. God was not pleased with this but nevertheless granted the people's wish. (Chapter 8)

Saul, from the tribe of Benjamin, was the divine selection to fulfill the role. Our first impression of the man is that he seemed to be a dutiful son, a humble farm boy. He also was a head taller than other men and exceptionally handsome.

Things were set in motion when Saul was sent by his father Kish to look for some lost donkeys. He didn't find them and was away so long that he was concerned his father would become worried about him instead of the lost donkeys, which may reveal a positive aspect of Saul's personality at the time. (Chapter 9)

The prophet Samuel was God's agent in the process of anointing Saul as king of Judah and remained in touch with the king through much of his reign, often instructing him and declaring God's judgments.

Those judgments came in due course. Saul's first recorded mistake occurred when, on the eve of a battle, he failed to wait for Samuel to arrive to offer the required sacrifice, and performed the rite himself. When Samuel did arrive, though late, he condemned Saul firmly for violating divine orders.

Next came more disobedience. After a victorious battle, Saul, against specific instructions, spared the enemy king and also captured as booty some of the foe's livestock. When Samuel discovered the violation, Saul compounded his sin by falsehood regarding the captured animals. (Chapter 15)

Then God spoke to Saul through Samuel: Because of disobedience, his kingdom would not stand. This did not mean instant abdication, but a successor king now would be selected and identified. It turned out to be David, a shepherd boy, the youngest son of Jesse. (Chapter 16)

Saul would reign many more years, even though the kingdom's end had been ordained, and there would be no succession to any of his sons. David by this time had become a fixture in the palace, playing musical instruments to soothe Saul's increasingly troubled mind. David also was a valiant warrior, so much so that he was given more credit among the people for victories than Saul himself, which led to the king's growing jealousy and resentment of the young man. (Chapter 18)

The deterioration of Saul became profound, causing him to consult a medium to raise the spirit of the then-dead Samuel. (Chapter 28) More than that, he sought to kill David, pursuing him relentlessly over a long period and forcing David to flee. Finally, Saul lost his life in battle, falling on his own sword. He had reigned forty-two years, a long but an essentially failed kingship. (Chapter 31)

That's the history in brief. What are the takeaways? Let's go back to the beginning. The people's desire for a king seemingly was outside God's perfect will but within his permissive will. Thus it was granted, which may lead us to the admonition: "Be careful what you pray for."

What was wrong with seeking a king? By doing so, the Israelites effectively were ceasing their dependence on God, but additionally they saw that other nations had kings and wanted to emulate the pagans and their cultures. That failing seems familiar in our own time within some Christian circles.

But why Saul? First, he was tall and handsome, just the kind of man people of shallow values would want in a political leader. Also, he was of the tribe of Benjamin. We have to believe the eventual bloodline to Jesus had already been established as coming through the tribe of Judah. Events had pointed that way long before the birth of Saul. The story of Boaz and Ruth is an example. (Ruth 4) So this first king, sought and granted outside God's perfect will, could not fulfill the divine plan, nor could he establish a dynasty.

The role of Saul in God's plan may rest in the life of David. Because of the king's failures, David was anointed the successor at an early age. (1 Samuel 16) Then still a lad, David encountered Goliath in a war between Saul's Israelites and the Philistines. (Chapter 17) The future king's rise to prominence and popularity ensued from there.

When Saul's envy turned to hatred of David, the king in effect lost his mind. Thus we might conclude that mental illness is not always organic or chemical but can be self-induced out of an evil heart, as in this case.

The scenario that played out forced David to take desperate measures to preserve his life. The situation also led him to demonstrate a remarkable loyalty to the king as God's anointed. On two occasions when his own life was in peril, David's spared Saul's, thus showing a large measure of godly mercy toward his adversary. (Chapter 26)

Did God cause Saul to go bad? No. That was the product of the man's own choices. Does God have a purpose that would be carried out? Yes. If we have trouble with that concept, meaning free will alongside inevitable outcome, we must remember we don't have the mind of God, as Isaiah 55 states.

So again, why Saul? One answer may be that Saul was necessary to lead the way to David, ordained to become king of Judah, the ancestor of Jesus. And it may be that even Saul's crazed pursuit of David's life had its own purpose in honing David's character, which was to build him into the man he would become, one after God's own heart.

THE WISEST MAN

S olomon, son of David and his successor as king of Judah, is mainly known for his wisdom. In fact, his name and that quality are virtually synonymous. That fact played a great part in the development of Solomon's life and informed much of his teachings.

Solomon is credited with writing three books of the Old Testament: Proverbs, Ecclesiastes, and Song of Solomon. It is the second of those works that reveals the most about the man Solomon and may provide the most telling lessons for mankind.

The first mention of the name comes in 2 Samuel 12:24 after the death of the infant son from the first encounter of David and Bathsheba. Solomon then became the first son to survive from the then-married king and Bathsheba, though he was not the oldest of all of David's sons.

As David lay near death, he designated Solomon as heir to the kingdom (1 Kings 1:43) presumably with approval by God. We must take note that it would not be this more prominent of David's sons who would provide the biological line to Jesus, but his obscure brother Nathan, rarely mentioned in David's family. It was during that time that palace intrigue arose. One of David's sons by another wife claimed the crown and managed to secure a substantial following. (1 Kings 1:5-7)

Enter Bathsheba, (1 Kings 1:17) who told the king of these events and intervened on behalf of her son Solomon. This move succeeded in restoring the anointed order of succession. On his deathbed, David instructed Solomon in different ways, (1 Kings 2:1-10) among them declaring that it would be Solomon who would build God's temple, a privilege specifically denied David for stated reasons.. He also laid out a plan of kingdom cleansing involving Joab and the man Shimei, a persistent nemesis to David during his lifetime.

Solomon as king accomplished the instructions in short order through death sentences, dealing in that manner also with his half-brother Adonijah the usurper. He also defrocked the priest Abiathar, thus demonstrating a hard resolve when necessary. (1 Kings 2:1-27)

But the seminal event at the outset of his reign came when Solomon offered his inaugural prayer to God. The humble young king, apparently daunted by the great responsibility placed upon him, prayed only for wisdom that he might rule Israel well.

The selfless prayer so pleased God that he not only granted the stated wish but also the unrequested material blessings of wealth and long life. (1 Kings 3:10-15) Thus Solomon would reign over a period of peace and prosperity. He would build the great temple and his own palace. Most of all he would be invested with such great wisdom that his name would forever be associated with that quality. Solomonic became an adjective.

Proof came quickly during his administration when two women claimed the same baby as their own. When Solomon suggested cutting the infant in half, the identity of the real mother was promptly revealed. Thus we still have in our language the phrase "dividing the baby" to describe the ability to solve a difficult problem. (1 Kings 3:16-26)

It was during the Queen of Sheba's visit to Judah (1 Kings 10) that the sheer splendor of the kingdom, as well as Solomon's impressive qualities, came into full view. The queen was so taken by what she witnessed there, with respect to both the man and his surroundings, that she hardly had the vocabulary to describe it.

That is why the very next chapter of 1 Kings catches us by surprise, because it is there that the apostasy of Solomon and his kingdom is shown. He had fallen into idolatry, his 700 wives and 300 mistresses included many of alien descent. This chapter records nothing positive about the man or his reign. To put it simply, despite all the favor God had shown him, all the blessings his kingdom enjoyed, all the sterling qualities with which Solomon had been endowed, at the end, it appeared he and his kingdom had failed.

The result was God's judgment. Solomon was told that the kingdom, the seat of David, would not stand in full, that only a remnant, the tribe of Judah (Benjamin also would join it) would remain. But God spared Solomon personal judgment, allowing him to live out his life before the kingdom was fractured through the separation of the 10 northern tribes into what would be known as Samaria. (1 Kings 11:9-13)

It is here that the final story of Solomon becomes difficult, he being blessed of God but ending in idolatry and hedonism. What can we conclude?

Perhaps it is the Book of Ecclesiastes, written toward the end of his life when he could reflect on it all, the good and the bad, that reveals the most. The early chapters may contain the central theme: Solomon had God-given wisdom; yet that alone was not enough. He had untold riches, yet they did not satisfy. He enjoyed great pleasure (1,000 women at his disposal), but that was not the answer. Solomon's repeated mantra was that all was vanity; all was futile.

The book contains many other thoughts: The inevitability of history repeating itself, the specific times set aside for specific purposes, the common end of all men, and even advice on how to achieve temporal enjoyment in life.

But finally, Solomon wrote that it came down to this central truth: Man must know and serve his God, no matter his gifts, great or small. Man is still accountable and can fall. (Ecclesiastes 12:13-14)

Perhaps we can understand a perspective on Solomon's life by considering the mysterious way God directs events, using human failure to his own purpose. For instance the breakup of the kingdom was the catalyst leading to captivity, thus spreading God's chosen, the Jews, throughout much of the world to the benefit of humanity and the propagation of the gospel.

FROM ICON TO IDOL

There are at least three significant Biblical references to the bronze serpent fashioned by Moses at the instruction of God, and within those we should find important teachings.

The initial mention is in Numbers (21:9), which records the disobedience of the children of Israel as they traveled toward the promised land after their exodus from Egypt. As the resulting judgment, God sent among the people poisonous snakes whose bite was lethal. And many Israelites died.

Then God offered a solution, telling Moses to make the bronze serpent and place it on a standard, apparently meaning somewhere at an elevation so it could be seen. Those Israelites suffering from snakebite could find deliverance from the venom simply by looking on the raised serpent. Many did so and lived, and though it was not stated in the scripture, we can suppose others did not obey, possibly in defiance but more likely viewing the instruction as too simple to be believed.

Has this same attitude been at work in the world since the time of Christ? Salvation by faith is no doubt seen by some as too easy to be true; such reasoning would conclude that there must be something more a man should do to be accepted into God's kingdom. Thus the bronze serpent, as a means of saving one's life, became a type and shadow of salvation by faith, and also an example of the human tendency of resistance to the free offer of grace and forgiveness.

Jesus made mention of the bronze serpent when he declared its Old Testament significance and its application to his own mission. "Just as Moses lifted up the snake in the desert, so the Son of Man must be lifted up." (John 3:14)

The bronze snake was placed high enough for people to see, just as Jesus was lifted above the ground at Calvary, but there is an important distinction. The serpent represented deliverance only from physical death, while Jesus fulfilled redemption from spiritual death.

To further the point, Jesus stated in another setting (John 12:32-33) that if he was lifted up, all men would be drawn to him. This may have a double meaning; first he referred to the kind of death he would suffer, including the physical elevation. But Jesus also may have meant that when his followers lifted up his name as Lord and Savior, the inevitable result would be attraction of willing believers, the name itself being a magnet..

Finally, we come to the negative side of the existence of the bronze serpent. It is found in 2 Kings during the reign of Hezekiah, king of Judah, one of the most righteous of those kings since the time of King David.

Most of Hezekiah's predecessors had been evil and had led their people into idolatry in various degrees as the history of the kingdom unfolded. So the good king set about the business was destroying the idols of worship, including the altars and Asherah poles, as some of his better predecessors had done.

However, in this case, Hezekiah also smashed to pieces the bronze serpent because the Israelites had been burning incense to it, thus making that object an idol as well. (2 Kings 18:4) It is not recorded whether this was the actual serpent that had survived from Moses' time or whether artisans had fashioned a replica later, but that make no real difference to the significance of the story.

If God's people of the old covenant could turn what had been intended as a means of deliverance into an object of idolatry, what might his people of the new covenant, meaning Christians, do?

Is it possible the incident recorded in 2 Kings was intended to teach us of the possibility of committing the same sin, that of worshipping a representative object rather than the person of the Lord to which the object is to point? These idols might include such a thing as the church building, a metal cross or any of the trappings of the faith that in themselves are good and worthy of respect for what they represent and the purpose they serve.

The bronze serpent when fashioned served a holy purpose in God's plan, which Jesus took pains to point out despite the wrong use the Israelites had later made of it. We could see its history as a cautionary lesson as well.

IMPERFECT HEROES

Many years ago, a newspaper executive addressing a class of journalism students made this comment: "One reason I know the Bible is true is because it is so objective about its heroes," meaning willingness to show warts and all. He said this to encourage those in his audience to display the same degree of the truthfulness in their work.

With that in mind, we'll examine a number of biblical characters to demonstrate the validity of the newsman's statement. None is this is a revelation to a Bible student, but it might be instructive to put the subject into one bundle and draw a general conclusion.

First up is Abraham, the father of nations and a champion of faith, as extolled in Hebrews 11. He told Egyptians his wife Sarah was his sister, thus putting her in peril but, he thought, protecting himself against the possibility of losing his life. (Genesis 12:11-13) In fact, she was his half-sister, but that buys him no credit. This was a case of a literal truth being a pure falsehood because it denied the more important reality.

Like father, like son. Isaac in his turn told the same lie (Genesis 26:7) regarding his wife Rebekah, and he did not have the benefit of the half-truth technicality as his father had.

Next comes Jacob, divinely ordained in the womb to be the child of promise instead of his older twin brother Esau. But he achieved that outcome by taking advantage of his brother and then falsifying his identity to his nearly blind father. (Genesis 27) Jacob, though the father of the 12 patriarchs, the children of Israel as God directed, did not distinguish himself as a husband or parent. He clearly favored one wife Rachel over the other, her sister Leah, and that favoritism spilled over to his sons. He doted on Rachel's son Joseph to the point that it poisoned the relationship between the brothers. (Genesis 37)

Jacob's fourth son Judah, not necessarily the prize among the 12, was to be the ancestor of Jesus. So what was the life of this son of Leah like? He began by marrying a foreign woman who bore him three sons, two of whom married a woman named Tamar but died early without leaving a male heir. Judah then decided to consort with what he believed to be a common prostitute, but who in fact was his own daughter-n-law Tamar. The result was the birth of twins, one of whom was Perez, the next in line that would lead to the Lord. (Genesis 38)

Moses the law-giver, Moses who led his people across the Red Sea and out of Egypt, Moses who shepherded a nation for 40 years in a journey to the Promised Land. Even this larger-than-life figure of scripture failed in a significant way. God ordered him and his brother Aaron to speak to the rock in order to bring forth water. They did not; instead an angry Moses struck the rock twice. God did not hold back the water; nor did he withhold his judgment on both. Aaron, who had committed the sin of omission by not speaking to the rock as instructed, would not live to see the land of Canaan. Moses, who had sinned both by commission and omission, received the greater punishment. He was allowed to see what he could not have, the promised land he had invested so much to reach.

We should not minimize Moses' transgression as a mere momentary burst of anger. His disobedience had usurped the glory of God by claiming it for himself. As for Aaron, he already had committed a serious trespass when he fashioned a golden calf while Moses was on the mountain, and then compounded the sin by making up a preposterous story that the calf had jumped out of the fire fully formed.

King David's sins of adultery and murder need no further detailing here. Two points can be made. He was tempted of Bathsheba because he was not where a king is supposed to be in time of war: with his troops. Instead, he was taking his ease at home. Second, his attempts to cover up the first act is a picture of the way sin by its very nature can grow, in this case from mere manipulation to the ultimate crime. In that sense, David was no less guilty than a Mafia boss who orders the assassination of a rival. (2 Samuel 11)

Jesus had an inner circle of apostles, Peter, James and John. The latter two were brothers, and on one occasion they allowed worldly personal ambition to take over. Their request to be given special places of honor in the kingdom was, by one gospel version, abetted by their mother, which made them appear even weaker. (Matthew 20:20-23) Besides the self-promotion being inappropriate, it came just after the Lord had told them of his impending suffering and death. So the brothers were totally tone-deaf also.

The Apostle Peter, that tough fisherman, is about the last man anyone would have suspected of denying Jesus, which he did three times. His failure came a short time after he was found sleeping when he should have been praying. But most important is that on the very same night Peter, full of pride, had boasted that he would follow his Lord to the death. That kind of self-confidence in one's own virtue can be a sin in itself. What price did Peter pay? Maybe that came when, after his denial, he and Jesus made eye contact: thus bitter remorse. (Luke 22:54-62)

Each of the 10 men whose lapses are described was totally and personally responsible for his own actions. Yet in a way that people cannot quite comprehend, we can conclude that such as this had to take place. Can we imagine how bereft of the lessons contained therein the Bible would be if David, Moses, Peter and the rest had lived perfect lives? And what are the central truths? One is that even the best of human beings can and will fail. More important still, as these cases show, the sins did not define their lives. God's grace, mercy, redemption, and validation were still very much in evidence.

BIBLICAL WOMEN

We start with recognition that the world of biblical times was male-dominated and patriarchal. Females were subordinated at almost every level. Counterbalancing that fact are accounts of strong, devout women whose experiences, if anything, are more intriguing than those of many men of the Bible. That is where our study will take us as we consider twelve women, three sets of fours.

The first set is of those women specifically named in Jesus' genealogy; the second four are those who experienced miraculous or at least highly unlikely pregnancies, and the last group was chosen because of lives that reflected certain qualities or experiences.

So we have Rahab, Tamar, Ruth and Bathsheba. Rahab the harlot was a Canaanite woman of Jericho who protected the Israelite spies (Joshua 2:1-4) and later married into the family of God to become the great-great grandmother of David. She was a godly woman by the time she became part of scripture but her past apparently was not so virtuous and the label of harlot remained with her as if it were part of her name.

Tamar (Gen. 38:14-18, 24-29), like all Israelite women of their time, simply wanted to bear a son and chose her former father-in-law Judah to be the father. Thus we have her disguised as a prostitute in a place where she knew Judah would be. The result, of course, was the birth of Perez, who would be in the direct line to Jesus. That was the fulfillment of God's plan, but one brought about by the most questionable of means.

Ruth's story is told in full in the Old Testament book by her name. The main point here is that she was a Moabite, who presumably once embraced the pagan gods of her land. By remaining loyal to her Israelite mother-in-law, she migrated to Israel, converted to Judaism, married Boaz and became the great-grandmother of David. She truly was a great woman of destiny.

Little more needs to be said about Bathsheba other than that she was once the wife of Uriah the Hittite, fell into adultery with David, married him and was mother to both Solomon, the successor king, and Nathan, an ancestor of Jesus.

So what do we make of these four women in Jesus' genealogy, two and possibly three of whom were not Israelites (was Bathsheba, like her husband, a Hittite also?) and three of the four having a history of sexual indiscretions. The ancestry may remind us that Christ is the savior of all people, not just those who have a pure moral or ethnic pedigree. But Christians generally know that, so what puts emphasis on this truth is that Jesus not only saves such as those but could count them as blood relatives.

No Jewish woman of the biblical times believed herself to be complete until she had borne a son, thus we have Sarah, Hannah and Elizabeth, all barren and advancing in age.

Abraham had been promised a son of destiny, but it wasn't happening and Sarah's faith failed her. She induced Abraham to father a son by her Egyptian maid (Gen. 16:1-2), an act Sarah would come to regret and one that apparently has changed world history. But the main point is that Sarah's failure did not cancel the promise, which eventually was fulfilled in their old age with the birth of Isaac.

(1Samuel 1: 11, 20, 28) Hannah was so desperate for a son that she made a deal with God by promising to dedicate the child wholly to spiritual service. Samuel became a great leader, thus redeeming Hannah's pledge. Hannah's husband, by the way, showed how clueless men can be by wondering why his wife (before her pregnancy) was so sad all the time.

Elizabeth, like the others, yearned to have a son but was all too aware of her biological clock. She was the wife of Zacharias, a Levitical priest, but he doubted the promise of a child and was struck dumb temporarily (Luke 1:13-15, 18-20). The birth of John the Baptist fulfilled the promise and it was Zacharias, the previous skeptic, who obeyed the angelic command by naming him John, contrary to Jewish and family tradition.

Sarah, Hannah and Elizabeth were all devout women who were blessed mightily by God but notice the contrast between them and the Virgin Mary when she was visited by Gabriel. Mary was a teenage girl; the others were of mature age. Their promise of sons, while beyond normal belief for those three women, nevertheless fell into the realm of natural process. A virgin birth was far different. Yet Mary immediately accepted whatever God had for her (Luke 1:35, 38). There was no faltering of patience, bargaining with God or outright disbelief, as was the case in some respects in the Old Testament instances.

Deborah qualifies for our discussion of significant biblical women because she represents such a sterling exception to the male domination of her time. As an Israelite judge during that period she in effect was a head of state; not only that, she was a warrior judge and a successful one at that, thus fulfilling every role otherwise reserved for men (Judges 4:4-9).

Leah, the first wife of Jacob, was the older, less attractive of two sisters (Gen. 29:16-17). Jacob always loved Rachel more and showed his preference clearly. For instance, when he and his entourage were about to meet his brother Esau, whom he feared might want to attack his party, he gave Rachel and her children more protection than Leah and hers (Gen. 33: 1). However, Leah gave Jacob his first four sons. After each of the first three was born, she hoped this would cause Jacob to love her. He didn't. So after number four, Judah, came along, Leah gave up on Jacob and turned her allegiance to the Lord instead (Gen. 29:31-34).

Judah, of course, was the patriarch through whom Jesus would come. So it should interest us that Leah, the less loved, should be chosen of God to be an ancestor of the Lord. Could this be the consolation prize for spending her entire married life in second place? It was more than that. And while neither Judah nor Leah could have known what would happen centuries later, it seems certain that Leah knows it now and understands the great privilege that was hers.

For Esther, the Jewish queen of Persia who saved her people from annihilation, it all comes down to one statement by her cousin Mordecai as recorded in Esther 4:14. To paraphrase that verse, the queen is told she may have been brought to that time, place and circumstance for that very purpose, but if she failed to act, someone else would. Of course she did not fail. Blessed is the person who could point to such a meaning to his or her life. Danny Thomas once remarked that he felt he was born to establish St. Jude's Children's Hospital; a Navy chaplain ministered to survivors of a sunken warship during World War II and finally sacrificed himself by giving his life jacket to a struggling seaman. His act, wrote the author of the book about the battle, was "what he had been put on earth to do." Maybe many ordinary Christians living ordinary lives have experienced a seminal event of that sort, without necessarily even knowing it.

Not much is written about a woman whose name is so well-known: Mary Magdalene. We know mainly that Jesus healed her from the throes of seven demons and that she became a devoted follower. But it was at Jesus' tomb that her earthly destiny was realized, because it was she, not Peter, not John, not any other apostle, but she who was accorded the honor of being the first person to see and greet the risen Christ, and further permitted to be the first to report that grand news to others (Mark 16:9-10). There must be great significance in that distinction.

By applying modern sensibilities on such matters, many might regard the Bible as hopelessly sexist. However, the twelve women we have discussed, as well as others we could add, certainly reflect a considerable amount of biblical truth. More than that, given the period of human history from which scripture is drawn, the word, instead of being dismissive of females, seems remarkably enlightened.

FULFILLING THE LAW

The relationship between the law first made known in the Old Testament and the concept of grace as central to the new covenant is such a deep subject as to defy any attempt to explain it here in any complete way.

However, Jesus' declaration that he came not to abolish the law but to fulfill it (Matthew 5:17) does open the door to a discussion even by laymen unschooled in theology. So the question at hand is this: What is meant by fulfillment of the law? And related to that is this: Which of the myriad Mosaic laws are still valid in the church age?

Let's start with the Ten Commandments, as listed in Exodus 20:3-17. We all know them. But when Jesus was asked about the greatest commandment, he boiled the ten down to two: Love God with all your heart, mind and soul, and love your neighbor as yourself (Matthew 22:34-40). Was the Lord merely striving for economy of expression, or was he saying something more? It seems it was the latter.

Notice the original commandments. Seven of the ten are prohibitions. "You shall not…." (Exodus 20:4, 7, 13-17). Contrast Jesus' words. He switches from negative to affirmative. That could make a significant difference.

To obey certain commandments before, a person would refrain from murdering his or her neighbor or stealing from the person. Jesus's command requires positive action if necessary. Loving a neighbor might mean doing a service for him or her, wishing the individual well, filling a need. It's the same with the First Commandment. It's one thing to recognize a single deity (no other gods before me) but another to serve God in worship and total commitment.

There are several ways to say this. The old emphasis was on the letter of the law; the fulfillment calls for embracing the spirit of the law. That idea permeates the teaching of Jesus and others.

Jesus, in describing the entire set of commandments in two sentences, made an even more profound statement when he said, "All the Law and the Prophets hang on these two commandments" (Matthew 22:40), meaning the entire Old Testament.

By distilling the Old Testament to a two-sentence summation of the Ten Commandments, Jesus seems in one way to have fulfilled the law as he said he would.

But there is more, especially as it regards two commandments, murder and adultery. These are sins of the heart and not only of action, as enunciated in Matthew 5. Hatred, malice, anger and contempt for another are not murder in themselves, but Jesus declares that the act starts there and anyone harboring those attitudes to a certain level cannot claim innocence under the Sixth Commandment. (5:21-22)

With adultery, his point is made even stronger. Lust in effect is the equivalent of adultery (5:27-28). Thus in both cases Jesus makes a clear statement of fulfillment, which is found in the spirit of the law and not only in its letter.

Two of the Ten Commandments, those regarding the sabbath and honoring of parents, were not negatively stated in the beginning, so their fulfillment is not as clear.

By saying that the sabbath was made for man and not man for the sabbath (Mark 2:27), Jesus appeared to lift the burden from the command and treat the concept as a blessing. Further, he himself became the Lord of the sabbath (Matthew 12:8).

The Fifth Commandment presents a stickier problem. We might dismiss it as dispensational, relating only to the time it was written. Then we could say that the promise to give the obedient long life could mean that Israelites who honored their parents' faith in God would be assured of an extended generational time in the Promised Land.

However, in Matthew 15:3-4 Jesus quoted the commandment (less the long-life promise) and added the Mosaic law requiring death for those who cursed their parents. We certainly know the Lord was not advocating that penalty for disrespectful children, but wanted to remind the Pharisees of how seriously the law viewed the relationship between parents and offspring. As for the commandment, we can believe that the principle applies in full force for Christians. That in itself is fulfillment.

Regarding the general Mosaic law, Jesus in effect canceled capital punishment for sin when he refused to allow stoning of the woman taken in adultery (John 8: 2-11). One takeaway from that encounter is this: Man does not have the moral authority to punish another's sin, by stoning or otherwise. Only in the theocracy of the Israelites was that possible. We do recognize that civil authority does punish crime as statutes permit.

The overall tone of the Sermon on the Mount, and indeed much of the New Testament, works to abrogate the laws of retribution prominent in the books of Moses. Jesus (Matthew 5:38) specifically singled out the "eye for an eye, tooth for a tooth" teaching of Exodus 21:24 by declaring that instead of getting even with those who harm or offend us, we should love our enemies, return good for evil, and so forth (Matthew 5: 38-42).

To oversimplify, maybe we can merely conclude that such Old Testament teachings as sacrifices and ceremonial taboos are to be left behind as nailed to the cross. But we also should recognize that the Mosaic law contained much wisdom and principles for living that are applicable to life today

Jesus and the law: He expanded it, superseded it, gave it new meaning, and personified it. In short, he fulfilled the law, as he said.

THE CHEERFUL GIVER

The subject at hand will be limited here so as not to include the broad aspects of our stewardship of Christian life or materialism in general, but will deal strictly with the biblical teaching about our monetary giving to the work of the Lord.

The matter of tithing naturally comes into play. The word is introduced in the Old Testament, but does not appear as a matter of obedience in the New Testament. But the idea can be seen as relevant in Christian life nevertheless.

The concept of making an offering to God comes at the very beginning when both Cain and Abel did so. Cain brought produce from the ground; Abel "fat portions from the firstborn of his flocks" (Genesis 4:4). His was accepted; Cain's was not. "Firstborn" may indicate "best"; no such description was made of Cain's offering, so there we may have the first principle of giving that pleases or displeases God. The unstated difference may also have been the attitude that accompanied the offering, a pertinence that is confirmed in later scripture.

That issue, in fact, arises at least as early as the book of Exodus (35:5) when gifts were solicited from the people to finance the building of the tabernacle. Moses wrote that the offerings should be made willingly.

It was back in Genesis that the tithe first appeared. After Abram (Abraham) defeated kings who had captured his nephew Lot and others, the mysterious figure Melchizedek appeared to him and received a tithe, literally meaning a tenth, from the patriarch (Genesis 14:18-20).

Paying the tithe may have been Abram's expression of gratitude for his success in freeing the captives. In Hebrews 7:8-11, the writer brings the tithe into the New Testament by referencing the event from Genesis and describing Melchizedek as the preincarnate Christ and thus still our object of allegiance and an appropriate recipient of the tithe from his followers.

The most salient Old Testament passage on the subject may be found in Malachi, who challenges the people with the question, "Will a man rob God?" (Malachi 4: 8) He then calls for the payment of "the whole tithe into the storehouse, that there may be food in my house." (Malachi 4:10) Two important principles are suggested here.

First, if withholding our tithes is robbing God, then the tenth belongs to him in the first place. Countless Christians hold to that truth when they contribute a tenth of their earnings to the Lord. It may go back to Abel's firstborn of his flock. No such quality can be ascribed to money, but priority can be. If the first tenth of income, and not the last, is devoted to the Lord as not belonging to the earner, that indeed may represent the offering without blemish.

The second truth is more practical. No matter how we may spiritualize the issue by saying God doesn't need our money because he owns it all anyway, which is true, the fact is that Malachi tells us our contribution has a temporal purpose here and now. If no one gives, the gospel won't be spread, the hungry won't be fed and so forth.

Jesus in Matthew 6:2-4 gives us a simple, but sound instruction about our gifts: Keep it between yourself and God. Don't make a show of it, which would expose a giver's motive to impress others about his generosity.

Wasn't that the problem with Ananias and Sapphira (Acts 5)? It wasn't that they didn't contribute the whole amount of the land sale, but had lied when they said they did. Peter reminded them that they had been free not to give it all, (5:4) which tells us that stewardship is a matter of conviction, not law. The couple's penalty indicates how seriously God takes such matters.

The final scriptural lesson to be dealt with here occurs when Jesus observed monetary gifts being made to the church. This is the well-known story of the widow's mite. This poor woman had only two small coins and gave both of them. The Lord took note that the wealthy had given out of their surplus, but she had offered more than all of them (Luke 21:1-4).

It is not difficult to discern the difference between sacrificial giving and its opposite. Jesus was not necessarily disparaging the generosity of the affluent in this case, but instead extolling the widow's faith and sacrifice by comparison.

So what do that passage and others add up to for Christians? First, we should know that tithing is not some kind of church tax. When people approach the issue with "What do I owe….." they are framing the issue wrongly, in my opinion. We also must acknowledge that many Christians of good will and understanding do not consider the specific tithe as the basis for determining their gifts.

Nevertheless, if we are seeking a numerical scriptural standard on stewardship, the teaching of tithing fits that description. Thus many Christians consider the 10 percent as a benchmark for determining the starting point for their offerings.

Monetary offering begins as a matter of faith and also of worship. Faith derives from the confidence in God's provision, and specifically the belief that, as Malachi states, the tithe belongs to the Lord and that the remaining 90 percent will suffice for the giver equally well.

The arrival of a godly, scriptural approach to monetary stewardship, no matter the amount or percentage, comes by faith and worship, and not by law or duty. We should find pleasure and fulfillment in giving that helps spread the gospel or meet human needs. At that point, a Christian can know what it means to be a cheerful giver as the Bible teaches.

MARRIAGE AND DIVORCE

Dealing scripturally with these two separate but related subjects leads us first into disagreement with current popular culture and next into revisiting an issue that long has divided people inside and outside the church world.

Until recent decades, definition of marriage was a given in the church and western society in general. Unfortunately that is no longer the case for reasons there is no need to describe here.

So for Christians, it's back to basics as to the scriptural standard for marriage. That is found in a single, simple verse (Genesis 2:24). Boiled down, it means one man, one woman, monogamous for life, a truth Jesus reiterated strongly in the gospels. While the wedding process was never spelled out fully in the Bible, we can know there was an identifiable way to determine whether a couple was married or not.

Jesus provided the answer to that in his encounter with the Samaritan woman at the well when he told her what she already knew: She had been married multiple times before but was not married to the man she was living with (John 4:16-18). So there was a clear distinction between wedlock and cohabitation in New Testament times. By inference we can believe that there were moral and legal implications as well.

We notice that Jesus neither commended nor condemned the woman for her lifestyle, but instead brought her to conversion and used that divorcee of checkered past to witness to her entire village.

This brings us to the matter of divorce as we observe it in our time and as the issue is addressed in the Bible. We can start with the proposition that the breakup of a marriage, whatever the reasons, is a distortion of God's ideal for human families.

The scriptures contain ample guidance with regard to divorce, in the gospels as well as in the Old Testament and in some of Paul's writings. These teachings can be seen as hard to apply in life situations, but not difficult to understand.

The strongest statement in the Old Testament is from Malachi 2:14-16, which admonishes men to treat the wives of their youth with consideration, concluding with the flat declaration that the Lord hates divorce.

Paul discussed the issue in 1 Corinthians 7, mostly with respect to how a Christian spouse navigates his or her marriage to a non-believer. Some denominations rely on passages in 1 Timothy 3:2 and 12 regarding qualifications for overseers (ministers) and deacons, taking the statement that such should be "the husband of but one wife" to mean that divorced men would generally be disqualified.

But the foundational passages on the subject are found in Matthew 19:3-9, and Mark 10: 1-11. They cover much of the same ground with variations. The Pharisees opened the discussion by asking Jesus whether a man may divorce his wife for any reason. Jesus directed them to the law of Moses, to which they responded that Moses in effect gave them permission (Deuteronomy: 24:1).

Jesus did not dispute their reading but did correct them as to the true principle by reminding them of the definition of marriage from Genesis and then exposing the Pharisees' real motive in asking the question. It was the hardness of their hearts, the same as afflicted their ancestors.. They apparently were seeking an excuse for easy divorce. During this time, the Jewish community was divided between two rabbinical schools of thought on divorce, one strict and the other lenient.

Lest Moses' seeming compromise gives us pause, let's consider that the passage gave Jesus his opening to emphasize the biblical standard for marriage and to declare clearly his doctrine on divorce and remarriage. Thus we might conclude that this fragment of Mosaic law, though subject to question, had its own scriptural purpose as a teaching occasion by the Lord himself.

We get the picture. There is one legitimate reason for divorce, and that is infidelity (Matthew 19:9). Without that exception, any remarriage by either party results in the sin of adultery (Mark 10:11-12). And of course, unlike other sins, which can be stopped, repented for, forgiven by God and relegated to the past, the adultery of unscriptural remarriage is a continuing, lifestyle situation that cannot be cancelled except by the death of one of the parties or another divorce, itself a disruption of family. Furthermore, it puts any Christian involved in such a situation in the untenable position of realizing the ongoing nature of the transgression without a reasonable way to stop it.

Backing up a bit, it is easy for us to conclude that the Bible, and specifically the Lord himself, condemns serial marriages, casual divorces, moving from one spouse to another with little or no real cause and generally the pathology of fluid commitments prevalent in our day.

But what about the other cases? We all know about them and some have experienced one firsthand. Typically, these might involve an essentially innocent spouse, perhaps the victim of abuse or some other intolerable indignity. He or she might need to leave that marriage and in due time find someone else who provides a good home for the partner and any children.

Within the unequivocal teaching of Jesus on the matter, can there still be found room for God's grace, which is capable of bringing something good out of what began as a breaking of his ideal plan and will? Personal convictions will vary on that point and those directly involved are accountable, but otherwise some matters are best left to the judgment of God.

LORD OF THE SABBATH

What do New Testament Christians believe about the Old Testament concept of sabbath and how should that influence our behavior toward it? The question does not lend itself to a simple answer.

We start with the Fourth Commandment, "Remember the Sabbath day by keeping it holy" (Exodus 20:8). If the law as referenced in the New Testament means nothing less than the Ten Commandments, we know it was not canceled by Jesus, only fulfilled.

Predating the commandments, of course, was the six-day creation of Genesis, after which God rested from his labors on the seventh day, the basis for the commandment and the sabbath day observed by Jews and some Christian groups today.

The emphasis of OT sabbath law was rest from work. However, the commandment required adherents to keep the day holy, which suggests something more than merely taking the day off.

As the Mosaic law developed and then was interpreted by later Jewish leaders, the sabbath was loaded down with so many rules that its observance became highly restrictive and hard to keep.

During Jesus' lifetime and subsequently, the Jewish observance of the sabbath has been marked by synagogue services, which we can say meets the requirements of keeping the day holy.

After the resurrection of Jesus and the onset of the church age, Christians at some point adopted Sunday, the first day of the week, as the new "sabbath" and its observance included primarily worship services, a tradition that has lasted apparently unbroken to this very day, and rightfully so.

While the worship aspect of Sunday observance hardly comes into question among Christians, many other doctrines and activities can be in doubt in light of the Fourth Commandment as well as the teachings of Jesus and others in the New Testament.

Jesus declared that the sabbath was made for man and not man for the sabbath (Mark 2: 27). This seems to relieve the burden of the sabbath prevalent in the Old Testament and brought forward by religionists in Jesus' time. Jesus called the sabbath (or Sunday) a blessing for us, something to be enjoyed, not a slave to. Of course one such blessing is relief from the daily grind of work, or perhaps other strictures on our lives. Another is worship and service to the Lord on that day.

The Lord's teaching on this point came when he was challenged by the religious leaders on what seemed a minor point (Mark 2:23-26). As Jesus and his disciples were walking through a field on the sabbath, some, being hungry, pulled grain from the growing crop and ate it. To the strict constructionists, this was a violation of the sabbath. Jesus begged to differ and reminded the critics that even King David satisfied his hunger by eating dedicated bread in the temple. Thus, the sabbath was made for man, not the opposite.

Jesus put an even finer point on the issue by deliberately healing people on the sabbath, an offense to the Pharisees. The Lord's question to them, whether it was lawful to do good or evil on the sabbath, hardly needed an answer (Mark 3: 1-5).

Paul wrote of those issues that Jesus nailed to the cross and thus were no longer applicable. (Colossians 2:14-17) One of those was the matter of holy days, in effect the sabbath, which was beyond the purview of man to judge in another Christian.

So where does all of this leave us with regard to observing our sabbath, (Sunday)? What is permissible and what is not?

We must remember that at one time, even our civic society bought into the spiritual value of the sabbath. Many states and communities had so-called Blue Laws, which restricted the amount of business that could be conducted on Sundays.

Those laws are basically gone now as society has become more permissive, and we Christians ourselves have tended to loosen our idea of what is permissible on the holy day, such things as attending movies or ball games.

Let's consider the matter of employment. There are a variety of convictions, ranging from refusal to accept any job requiring Sunday work, to no compunction at all. Some might take a middle ground, allowing Sunday employment when required, but not purposely seeking ways to earn extra on that day.

We can't say anyone in the three examples is wrong in his or her conviction, which speaks to the principle of Christian liberty under the cover of grace. It also might apply to different issues, as Paul points out in Colossians.

He teaches also that all things are lawful for him but not necessarily useful. He wrote specifically about eating meat sacrificed to idols, which was not a sin unto itself but might offend a weaker brother. The same thing can be applied to the sabbath. Suppose a Christian wanted to wash the car or mow the grass on Sunday. One's liberty would allow that, but he or she might refrain for fear of offending a neighbor who might be a new Christian or one who is seeking.

When Jesus described the greatest commandment as loving God with all heart, soul and mind (Matthew 22:37), he surely embraced the Fourth Commandment, meaning that it still applies, not as a set of rules to bind us but as integral to our Christian faith. Thus we have the statement, "So the Son of Man is Lord even of the Sabbath" (Mark 2:28), which could be taken to mean that if our relationship with the living Christ is on a solid foundation, our relationship with the sabbath is likely to be also.

ALL ARE TEMPTED

The first point in understanding the important issue of temptation is to know that Jesus himself experienced it. Accounts of that event are recorded in both Matthew and Luke, and its purpose is confirmed by key teachings in the book of Hebrews.

There are further, significant truths about temptation in James 1:13 and 1 Corinthians 10:13. James writes quite plainly that God does not tempt and cannot be tempted, so that issue can be settled in our minds.

Paul in Corinthians makes two main points. First he tells us that all temptation is common to mankind. That is not to say we all have the same weaknesses that lead to temptation to the same degree but that in a broad sense, across the board, we can be sure all share the same class of temptation with just about everyone. Paul's second point is that no temptation is irresistible, as much as we might think otherwise. God, the apostle points out, will provide the strength to overcome any temptation.

We should acknowledge that while God does not tempt he does test his servants. Those tests may so resemble temptations as to be nearly indistinguishable and may even stem from the same circumstance. But we can know this: God tests to strengthen and purify. Satan tempts to lead people into sin and destruction. That's the difference.

We turn now to Hebrews, where the writer in one verse (4:15) makes the clearest statement about the reason Jesus was tempted. He did so in order to fully identify with the human race. He did not present himself only as a high priest who could not know what people experience. Lest we believe the accounts we are about to study in the gospels are merely an exercise in which Jesus went through the motion of temptation, Hebrews tells us that the Lord was tempted on all points, just as we are.

The verse in Hebrews ends with the statement that Jesus, though tempted, did not sin. Though it seems hard to separate temptation to sin from actually committing the sin, we can hardly imagine the Son of God reaching the point of desiring to sin. So there must be another truth to the matter, which we will try to deal with.

The biblical account of Jesus' temptation is found in the two gospels' fourth chapter. The versions are quite similar but with a variation at the end of each that is noteworthy. The narratives begin with the fact that Jesus had fasted for forty days, so he obviously was more vulnerable to Satan's wiles, an important point for our understanding of Jesus' ordeal.

Satan is shown as present with the Lord and his first temptation is of food, telling Jesus that as the Son of God he has the power to turn stones into bread. We can imagine that smooth, white rocks would resemble baked bread, especially to one who is famished. Jesus replies with scripture from Deuteronomy 8:3 that "Man does not live on bread alone but on every word that comes from the mouth of God." (Matthew 4:4) But is that all there was to it? Does it not seem likely that Jesus, for a moment at least, would at least consider the possibility? He knew he could accomplish the act, and might even have rationalized that doing so could be justified in the interest of his ultimate mission. But of course he did not.

The second temptation in Matthew was the inducement to jump from the highest point of the temple in the assurance that angels would save him from injury. In this case, Satan also quotes scripture, specifically part of Psalm 91, but the message of that passage would not justify what Satan proposed. Once again, the appeal to Jesus might have been that such an act would quickly establish his deity and his relationship with God the Father and thus accelerate his ministry. Jesus' answer was scriptural once again, telling Satan that we are not to put God to the test..

Satan then promised Jesus the entire world in exchange for the Lord's worship. This too was an appeal to expedience in Jesus' lordship and completing the plan of salvation. Perhaps Jesus considered for a moment that if he accepted the bargain, he could deal with Satan later. Of course the question remains: Was the world Satan's to give? In one sense, the devil is said to be the god of this world, so maybe he could have delivered.

Jesus's reply established his allegiance to the heavenly Father, and at that point, he dismissed Satan from his presence. In his dealing with the evil one, Jesus set an example for all of us by using scripture to counter the temptation.

We are reminded again of the statement in Hebrews, that Jesus was tempted on all points just as we are. Thus we are left with the conclusion that within the three temptations described in the gospels, or perhaps in subsequent visits by Satan, are contained all the classes of temptations one might experience.

Turning stones into bread might account for yielding to any human appetite; throwing oneself off a high place might expose the sin of presumption and pride; accepting Satan's offer of the world itself could bring the idea of personal power into play. As stated before, we are reluctant to put the sinless Jesus in quite the same position we find ourselves, in that temptation reveals a desire to sin. In his case, maybe we leave it this way: that the possibility and implications of Satan's bargaining could have crossed the Lord's mind, which would amount to temptation, before he then dismissed them as wrong and counter to scripture.

Luke's version of the subject describes Satan as leaving Jesus "until an opportune time," indicating he would return and perhaps tempt Jesus again. (Luke 4:13). The only hint of that came late in Jesus' ministry when he once again commanded Satan to depart.

As a final point, Matthew's account has angels coming, probably to offer food and otherwise minister to Jesus after the temptation (Matthew 4:11), thus putting to rest the notion this was just a game, a matching of wits between the Lord and the devil. This was real temptation, and it surely was an ordeal to be endured.

BLESSED ARE....

We can assume that since Jesus began his landmark message, the Sermon on the Mount, with what are commonly called the Beatitudes, they must be important. Important yes, and often quoted in whole or in part, but not so easy to understand.

As we know, all nine of the Beatitudes (Matthew 5:3-11) begin with the word, "Blessed," which often is defined as "happy," but which likely has a deeper spiritual meaning in this case.

For the central theme of the study I will borrow from the teaching of the passage that has most impressed me. It was done by a lady (unknown to me) over the radio. Briefly, she held that the Beatitudes represented a progression of the Christian life, starting with poverty of spirit and ending with such spiritual maturity that one would endure persecution and slander for his faith and count them as blessings.

"Blessed are the poor in spirit, for theirs is the kingdom of heaven." (Matthew 5:3) It is those who recognize their spiritual emptiness, and thus their need for redemption, who can gain salvation. Awareness of sin in one's life is the first step, but the end, as the verse declares, is heaven.

"Blessed are those who mourn"..."they will be comforted." (Matthew 5:4) It is no doubt true that Christians have a consolation in grief that cannot be attained by others, but the larger point here may be that a person, once aware of his or her sins, will mourn for having committed them, knowing of the pain they may have brought to others and the damage done to oneself. But the promise is for relief from that burden with the assurance of forgiveness.

"Blessed are the meek.…..they will inherit the earth." (Matthew 5:5) This is a little hard to fit into the progression of faith, but the message seems to contrast the humble, gentle, caring spirit with what the natural world believes is the key to success and acceptance: boldness, aggression, self-confidence, a sort of swagger through life. In the end, it will be the former not the latter who will prevail in matters that count. This is a fundamental truth that a Christian may in due time come to realize. Which persons whom we know of actually inherited the earth (and heaven) ? Bonhoeffer or Goebbels? Mother Teresa or Madalyn O'Hair?

"Blessed are those who hunger and thirst after righteousness…they will be filled." (Matthew 5:6) It could be a mark of Christian growth to develop a heightened desire for the word and for more righteous personal living. In this, God promises fulfillment.

"Blessed are the merciful, for they will be shown mercy." (Matthew 5:7) It is easy to believe that a truly forgiving spirit may take some time in coming to the newly converted, but when it does, the person has a fresh appreciation of the mercy God has shown him or her.

"Blessed are the pure in heart…." (Matthew 5:8). This might be another point of progression, when the maturing Christian realizes that his hidden thoughts and underlying disposition matter at least as much as his outward action. That is a definition of being "pure in heart" and there will be spiritual reward to follow.

"Blessed are the peacemakers…"(Matthew 5:9). This could refer to those who mediate trouble, who have a calming influence where needed, and so forth. But possibly the main point is that a peacemaker is one who seeks the reconciliation of a sinner with God, in other words a Christian witness. And when a believer is actively in that business, we have to say he or she has reached a special level of Christian maturity irrespective of the timing of conversion.

The eighth Beatitude blesses the Christian who suffers persecution as a result of his or her faith. The reward for that is exactly the same as that stated for poverty of spirit: "For theirs is the kingdom of heaven." (Matthew 5:10) So Christian faith, whether it comes early or late, whether one lives long or more briefly, brings forth the same ultimate reward.

The final Beatitude resembles the one before, but perhaps with two significant distinctions. Jesus may elevate it by adding slander to the suffering of the faithful, which may actually be more devastating than other persecution. Jesus also connected a Christian's ordeal in the world to he himself; "…because of me," the scripture says (Matthew 5:11). So here we may see the best mortal man can achieve. Note that where reward in heaven is referenced as a given, the emphasis is on earthly joy. It may be that the quality of Christian life indicated in this Beatitude is its own reward, plus the one assured in eternity.

Here in a few short verses the Lord appears to describe the essence of the Christian life, from its origin with the conviction of sin, to its ultimate potential, with steps of progress in between, not necessarily in exact order and certainly not applicable in all cases.

But the idea of individual growth and process seems valid in the reading of the Beatitudes. There is a sense of order. It is doubtful that Jesus would have put together a random series of verities with no thought to how they would fit together. What follows in Chapters 5 through 7 is the Sermon on the Mount, a firm foundation for Christian living, the bedrock of which are the nine Beatitudes.

TALKING TO GOD

The practice of praying to God is so engrained in the life of a Christian that it might seem that no biblical study of it is necessary. But questions still arise and the scripture still has much to remind us of regarding the subject.

It should be noted that nearly everyone prays in some manner or times, including the nominal believer or even the non-believer. In an extreme situation, it seems human nature itself will lead someone to cry out to God for help or deliverance. "No atheists in the foxholes," is one way to put it.

The most basic biblical teaching on the subject is what is commonly called the Lord's Prayer, but more properly should be known as the model prayer (Matthew 6:9-13). In it, Jesus points to some essential elements that should be included in a prayer, starting with recognition of who and where God is and that he is worthy of our worship ("hallowed be your name" (Matthew 6-9). Next comes our stated desire that his will is to be done in heaven and on earth, an important point we will deal with further on.

The petition to "give us today our daily bread" (Matthew 6-11) indicates our need for faith that God will care for us. When manna fell for the Israelites, they were instructed to gather it only for that day and not the next. They would need faith that he would provide the next day too, and that idea seems to be at work in the daily bread plea in the model prayer.

The prayer also connects forgiveness of others with our own need for the same, and asks that God lead us away from temptation. The prayer's close is another stated recognition of the majesty and glory of God the Father.

Not every element of prayer life is included in the model prayer, but other teachings through the New Testament fill in what we might call the important points, such as intercession, thanksgiving, persistence, and the need to approach the matter with the right attitude, among other things.

Jesus had something to say about the last when he contrasted the prayer of the Pharisee with that of the publican, a tax collector who by definition would be regarded as a notorious sinner (Luke 18:9-14). The Pharisee's prayer was self-righteous and judgmental; the publican's humble plea asked only for mercy. The Lord was quite clear about whose prayer was heeded.

In the same vein, Jesus also warned against praying conspicuously if the motive is to draw attention to one's piety (Matthew 6:5-6).

The book of James touches on the subject is different ways. First, he indicates that some by the sparseness of their prayer life leave potential blessings on the table. "You do not have because you do not ask God," James wrote (James 4:2). Next he condemns, as Jesus did, what he calls wrong motives in prayer. What might wrong motives be? Perhaps he had in mind selfish prayers that don't consider the needs of others. For instance an employee might pray for advancement in his company, but suppose he is in competition with a colleague. What is good for one man is less fortunate for the other.

James calls for intercession (James 5:14-15), an important element in prayer in which most Christians no doubt participate, either privately or corporately. A survey once found that people who pray for their own health recovery have a higher rate of improvement, not surprising in that prayer might be therapeutic in itself. But what was remarkable in that same study was that those for whom others were praying also fared better.

The need for persistence in prayer was most illustrated by the parable told by Jesus of the widow and the unjust judge (Luke 18:2-8). If that judge without compassion or morality responded to her repeated petitions, how much more would a loving God do so? So the lesson is this: Don't give up even when it seems prayers are not being answered.

The reality of God's will may be the most intriguing aspect of personal prayer. Jesus, on the worst night of his life, prayed to God to be spared his coming ordeal, but immediately yielded in obedience. "Yet not as I will but as you will." (Matthew 26:39) Perhaps he was telling us by that example that God is open to hear our most strident prayer, but we must accept another outcome according to his will.

The Bible tells us that God already knows our needs, which raises this question with many: Then why pray? The answer starts with the reality of God's will, which may be unchanging in any given circumstance. But then again, it might not be, meaning that God's will can be actuated from prayers sent up from one or perhaps many of his followers. We can't discount that possibility.

The matter of faith comes in, not as our confidence that our petition will be answered in the way we hope, but that God's perfect will is to be done, and we place our confidence in that fact, as hard as that may be at times.

James also tells us that "the prayer of a righteous man is powerful and effective" (James 5:16). We can take it from that teaching that a person's spiritual position and the earnestness in which the prayer is offered make a difference.

One of the questions that arises at times is this: Which prayers does God hear or not hear? It is not a question we can answer, but it would be a mistake to limit God's capacity. The desperate plea by a secular human to a deity he does not know may indeed be heard and be the first step toward the person coming to fuller knowledge of the Lord.

The references cited above do not exhaust the scriptural content on the subject of prayer. Perhaps what we need to know most of all is the instruction to be in prayer, understanding that the very exercise of it, in effect conversation with God, bears its own spiritual fruit whatever the specific answer to a petition might be.

BORN BLIND

The ninth chapter of John opens with Jesus encountering a man who was blind from birth, and one or more of the apostles asking what for them was a perfectly natural question: Who sinned to cause this, the son or his parents? To them, it had to be one or the other (9:1-2).

If the apostles had studied the book of Job, they should have known better than to make such an assumption, because it was just that belief that caused the three so-called friends of Job to conclude that the calamity that had come upon him could be explained in no other way than punishment for his sin. So it is somewhat surprising that the same idea persisted in Jesus's time and even more so that there are vestiges of it today.

The Lord's response was direct (9: 3). No one had sinned, but the man's blindness would allow the works of God to be demonstrated. Thus it appears Jesus was saying that the man's disability had a precise meaning from the beginning so that his eventual healing would bring glory to God.

This is a single instance recorded in the gospel. What about others who have suffered physical misfortune either by accident or natural causes? When a tower fell and killed 18 people, Jesus was asked whether the victims were worse sinners than any others. Briefly, his answer was no.

Let's consider the case of Joni Eareckson Tada, who has been wheelchair-bound since the age of 19 due to a diving accident. At present, and for many years, Joni has been a powerful witness for Christ, well-known throughout the Christian world. Would that have been the case had she lived what we would call a normal life? Maybe not. Did God cause her accident? We certainly are not prepared to believe that. But did he use the circumstance for his glory, and for her own good as well? So it seems.

The point is that God can use any situation, even one seemingly tragic, whether by divine design or the vagaries of life, for his own good purpose. Romans 8:28 tells us that "in all things God works for the good of those who love him…"

We can't leave this study, however, without recognizing that sin is not always unconnected to the afflictions that might beset us. Sometimes they come as a direct consequence of our acts or what others might do to us. The principle of divine discipline is also clearly taught in the Bible.

Returning to John 9, we notice that unlike other healing incidents, which usually are dealt with briefly, this one consumes the entire chapter and provides other lessons along the way.

First, there was considerable discussion in the area, with some people not even believing this man was the one who had been blind (9: 8-10). The Pharisees also disagreed among themselves about the legitimacy of Jesus' action (9: 16-18); and those who opposed Jesus's ministry made every effort to disprove the healing. Thus we have a look at the reaction to Jesus and the gospel that carries over into the present world. We see division and doubters and those hostile to the Christian faith doing all they can to discredit the Bible's message.

The man's parents are brought into the discussion, and they, unfortunately, showed weakness (9:20-23). Fearing they would be banished from the synagogue, they would not openly declare that it was

Jesus who had given their son sight. This reaction represents those who would shrink from the truth for purely temporal, selfish considerations.

Next we see the man himself being challenged by the skeptical Pharisees, and he replies with what can be taken as the only testimony available to him at the moment (9:25). He knew only one thing for certain: He had been blind and now he could see. There was no arguing with that fact, just as those who testify as to what Christ has done for them cannot be contradicted.

Jesus approaches the formerly blind man again and offers him salvation if he will believe. The man does believe, which completes the Lord's work on his behalf (9:35-38). So we see that the healing of blindness in itself did not save the man, and conversion was a separate act.

As his last act in this drama, Jesus turns his attention to the Pharisees and points out their own spiritual blindness, which blocks their pathway to true sight (9:39-41).

To return to the original proposition: Here we have a man whose whole mission in life apparently was to live as a blind man until the Son of God encountered him and gave him sight. Does that sound cruel or unfair? Suppose we could ask that man the same question. Is there any doubt he would say that the blessing of sight after a life of blindness was sweeter still than what most of us take for granted. But more than that, with meeting the Lord, believing and finding redemption, he would say yes, he had gotten the best of life's bargain.

LESSONS IN HEALING

The gospels record many instances of healings by Jesus, all having that singular result in common. However, each incident, it seems, has a unique teaching of its own apart from the healing itself.

We will look at three of those situations in seeking to discover some less obvious truth that may be taught us.

Let's start with the demoniac living in the tombs (Mark 5:1-20), a man beset by evil spirits, which caused him to be unmanageable, self-destructive, and probably a danger to others. Jesus drove the spirits out, sent them into a herd of swine, restored the man's sanity and, more important, saved his soul. The pigs, of course, drowned themselves because of the evil spirits. It is what happened after all of those events that should interest us.

We see that the community became aware of what had happened and urged Jesus to leave the area (Mark 5:14-17). The scripture records the people's fright, but we also can assume they realized they had suffered serious economic damage with the loss of the herd and saw Jesus as the cause. There you have the values of the sinful world, one without God, one unconcerned about the redemption of a fellow man and distressed instead about material loss..

The healed demoniac wanted to leave with Jesus but the Lord said he should remain with his people as a witness to his salvation (Mark 5:18-20). Little is told us from that point on, but we must conclude that his testimony bore fruit; otherwise the scripture would not have included Jesus' instruction.

And from that comes the key point of the lesson. The townspeople, those who believed, came to realize that they had received a prize far more precious than the monetary value of their livestock. They now knew that visitation by Christ, rather than being a burden on them, was a matchless blessing, as always.

Next we come to the paralytic who was lowered down through the roof (Mark 2:1-5). The focus here is not on the man who was healed but rather on the four who brought him. They apparently had learned that Jesus would be teaching in town that day in someone's home and they decided to get their helpless friend to the Lord, assuming he could restore his health.

When they saw the crowd in and around the house, they knew they could not get inside through the door. At this point, we see the hearts of these men, because it would have been easy, and perhaps natural, for them to give it up for that day with apologies to the paralytic. I can put myself in that position. I might have congratulated myself on the effort at having at least tried and then returned home to watch television or something. Not these four. They were determined no matter what to get their friend to Jesus. Imagine what they had to do: Get a ladder and ropes, maneuver a grown man on a stretcher onto a roof, break through the tiles to create a hole perhaps six feet long, and lower him to the floor.

No wonder it was the faith of these four that Jesus saw (Mark 2: 5) and then told the man on the pallet, whose own faith was apparent, that his sins were forgiven. What's the lesson here? It matters much for anyone undertaking a witness for Christ whether he is merely going through the motions or truly cares about a person's soul. The four men described above cared a great deal and the results speak for themselves (Mark 2: 6-11).

In John 5, we come to the pool of Bethesda.. Many sick and afflicted people were gathered at the pool waiting for the waters to be stirred, at which time Jesus approached one of them and asked this odd question: "Do you want to get well" (John 5:6)? We might have expected the disabled man to reply with a resounding "Yes." Instead he offered an excuse as to why, after 38 years as an invalid, he had received no cure. No one, he said, had been able to get him into the water in time (John 5:7).

Jesus's question and the answer suggest strongly that the man did not really want to be healed, but enjoyed giving the appearance of trying. Why would anyone resist healing? It's not hard to believe someone might become comfortable in disability. The condition fosters sympathy, brings attention to the sufferer and most of all, insulates him from any demands on his life. No one should expect anything from him.

But Jesus healed the man. Unlike most other such instances, there is no mention of faith or the forgiveness of sins, just physical restoration. With that, Jesus slips away in the crowd, leaving the now-well man unaware of who had healed him (John 5:8-13).

The next act in this drama occurs when Jesus looks up the fellow again and in effect tells him is time to deal with his spiritual condition. "See, you are well again. Stop sinning or something worse may happen to you" (John 5:14. There would be no more hiding behind his disability.

These are three events in the ministry of Christ, having in common divine healing, yet each different in an important way. The first reversed a whole community's callous self-centered values, the second showed that Christian ministry is more than a gesture that gets your good-works ticket punched, and the third demonstrated God's sovereignty and wisdom in finding within a crowd just the one person who most needed his touch at that moment.

BROTHERS OF JESUS

When Jesus from the cross entrusted his mother Mary to the care of the "disciple whom he loved" (John) (John 19:26), does that not raise a question about her own sons and daughters, Jesus's half-siblings? Were they even there? And if not, why not?

Underlying that event may be an issue that is troubling the modern church in our own country -- and that is what most evangelicals would agree is the disappointing number of converts to Christianity in any given year.

Let's return to the New Testament. In John 7: 3-5, Jesus's brothers urged him to go to Jerusalem for a special event. They are described as non-believers and seemingly wanted only to enjoy the reflected glory of a brother who could perform miracles.

This passage may help answer the questions posed at the outset. Either the brothers did not care enough even to show up with their mother on such a critical day, or Jesus would rather have had his follower John instead of unbelieving flesh-and-blood to be the caregiver of his mother.

But doesn't all of this seem strange? Here James, Jude and the rest grew up in a household headed by the righteous man Joseph and a mother who as a virgin had borne the Son of God. Further, they could look up to an older brother who by the age of 12 (or earlier) had shown the initial signs of his destiny as Messiah. Would not early conversion of the entire family been assumed? Apparently not.

We come to the incident in Jesus' hometown (Matthew 13:53-58). In the local synagogue the congregation is first amazed at the scholarship and wisdom of Jesus, whom they knew only as the carpenter's son, once a resident of the community, and probably a carpenter himself. The crowd later became furious with him over one of his teachings (Luke 4:25-30). The point is that Jesus was scarcely accepted in his home city, as he later explained.

Unbelieving brothers? Hostile home folks? Little ministry progress in Nazareth? What does it add up to? Maybe it is this: Too much familiarity, which brings us back to the question for our time.

The slow growth in baptisms in an affluent, educated, advanced society may be the result of the gospel having lost its freshness among the people. Generally, the saved and unsaved alike know about Jesus, know the central points of the scripture, know there are Christian churches everywhere. Many unconverted may attend one of them. Bibles abound; most homes would have one or more. So a spokesman for Christ, no matter how eagerly one wants to share the gospel, may be hard-pressed to tell anyone anything he or she has not heard before. To such people, it's not really news at all, much less good news.

The word, then, likely finds more ready acceptance in virgin territory, whether it is a remote, primitive area or a populous, advanced one. Of course, we long have had missionaries doing fruitful work in such places. It's not hard to imagine how the message of salvation, perhaps for those who are hearing it for the first time, might indeed be the good news they welcome.

Something of that idea is expressed in the book of Ezekiel when the prophet is instructed by the Lord to testify to his own people, who, he reminded Ezekiel, are "hardened and obstinate." (Ezekiel 3:7) He was told he would find more acceptance if he were to prophesy to people of an alien language and nationhood.

You'll find no suggested antidote to the matter here. I would not be so presumptuous as to propose one, or even to insinuate that the American church is in any flawed. It must be noted that there are many dynamic churches in the land, led by dedicated pastors and filled with congregants who love the Lord. But it could be a case of arriving at a point when our society becomes the product of past evangelistic successes, where the Christian message is generally familiar and the scripture is available almost universally.

We might look at Europe where Christianity once flourished but now is hardly visible, where some cathedrals are converted to museums, among other signs indicative of a society gone almost totally secular. That continent is much farther along the same downward road that we now find ourselves.

The New Testament story ends well. James and Jude, at least, were converted at some point. Both wrote scriptural epistles. And James, as head of the church at Jerusalem, was instrumental in easing the way for Gentiles to be accepted without circumcision (Acts 15:13-14, 19).

So despite the overall negative outlook related to declining church attendance and lower conversion numbers, dare we strike a note of hope? If America passes one or two generations where humanism, secularism and other godless pathologies prevail, a point at which Europe already has arrived, both continents may yet become like virgin mission fields receptive anew to the promise of the gospel message, just as eventually happened to James and Jude.

THANKS BE TO GOD

The virtue of gratitude for favor or good fortune is one cultivated and practiced generally by people of civility. It also is a Christian value taught clearly in the scriptures. Lack of appropriate thankfulness, especially for the blessings of God, would reveal a serious deficit in a spiritual life.

Jesus himself set an example on at least two occasions. When he fed the 5,000 with what started as two fish; and five loaves, he first offered thanks to the Father, thus establishing, we can suppose, the precedent for table grace (Matthew 14:19).

Before the Lord raised Lazarus from the dead, he first lifted his voice to God in thanks, not for himself but for the benefit of those who heard. This, we might surmise, was an early example of public, corporate prayer.(John 11:41-42).

One of the difficulties in dealing with this subject is separating the expression of gratitude from the real thing. We do it all the time in real life, tossing off "thank you's" liberally whether we mean it or not, mainly as a courtesy.

We may do something of the same in our prayer habits, thanking God more or less as a ritual for whatever might come to mind that seems good in our life. It's not a matter of insincerity, just depth of feeling. Even at meal time, those of us who have never gone truly hungry nor had doubts about the availability of food may have trouble giving more than perfunctory thanks for what is put before us.

But the Lord knows the nature of our thankfulness. The best biblical example on the subject comes with the healing of the 10 lepers (Luke 17:11-19). They called out to Jesus seeking mercy. He responded by healing them, and then sent them away to present themselves to the priest for confirmation that they were no longer unclean.

The central point comes when one of the lepers returns to thank Jesus for the blessing of being made well. Jesus takes note of the fact that the other nine did not do so. Thus it becomes clear that the lack of appropriate gratitude for God's blessing is viewed seriously by the Lord.

In this instance, he tells the healed leper that "your faith has made you well" (Luke 17: 19). This leaves the strong impression that the other nine as insufficiently grateful were healed in body only, not spiritually.

A secondary teaching arises from this incident when the Bible noted that the thankful leper was a Samaritan. Once again, as in the famous parable, it is a member of the supposedly inferior racial group that is shown in a favorable light in contrast to others. Is there any doubt how God views an attitude of racial prejudice?

Of course it is possible to be thankful for the wrong thing. Consider Jesus' teaching about the two men who went up to the temple to pray, a Pharisee and a publican. The former, unlike the penitent tax collector, thanked God he was not like other (less worthy) men, even like that publican. He apparently was sincerely thankful but it earned him no credit with the Lord (Luke 18:10-14).

Spiritual gratitude offered even in the face of adversity can be especially meaningful. In such times, if we look deeply enough, we often can find something in the situation for which to thank God.

The story is told about Matthew Henry, the great 17th Century biblical scholar whose commentaries continue to be referenced in

Christian circles. He was once robbed on the street, obviously not a favorable circumstance, but he found reason to be thankful for four things.

First, he was grateful he had not been robbed before, second, that only his purse and not his life had been taken, third, that though his purse had been taken, it did not contain much, and fourth, that he was the victim of the crime and not the perpetrator.

The last of those may resemble the mindset of the Pharisee above, but there is a major difference. The Pharisee's gratitude was born of arrogance and belief in his moral superiority. Matthew Henry's grew out of compassion for an unfortunate fellow human who had chosen the wrong path.

"There but for the grace of God go I," Henry may have thought. It is a truth that any number of us could express at times.

The idea stems from the reality that except for certain good fortune that has come our way, nothing less than a gift from God, we might be the one in the gutter, or in prison, or in some other wretched circumstance.

It is when we can thank God for our deliverance from sin and its consequences, both in this life and the next, that gratitude becomes real and strong. It is heartfelt when we thank him for salvation, the Christian life and all that goes with it. After that, sincere thankfulness comes naturally for all the rest of our blessings, our families, health, provision, and even the air we breathe each day.

SADDUCEES' QUESTION

We don't know a lot about the Sadducees except that they represented one party among the Jewish establishment during the time of Jesus, the other being the Pharisees. What separated the two was the teaching of the resurrection of the dead, which the Sadducees denied.

Let's keep that fact firmly in mind as we read an account in the gospels, for example Mark 12:18-25. The Sadducees, in talking with Jesus, presented a scenario they hoped would trap him into a contradiction of some sort.

First they accurately described the Mosaic law that would require the brother of one who had died childless to marry the widow and father one or more children in the dead man's name.

That being the case, they continued, what about a (hypothetical?) woman who had consecutively married seven brothers, and was widowed by all without the issue of a child. Whose wife would she be in the resurrection?

Seemingly, the Sadducees hoped Jesus would be so stumped by such a circumstance that he would have to back away from his own teaching of resurrection and eternal life. And remember, they were employing a premise in which they themselves did not believe.

Of course, Jesus let his critics know that it was they, not himself, who did not know what they were talking about, and it gave him the opportunity to enunciate an important truth about heaven. Whatever else we might discern from the scripture about the nature of eternal life, it is clear there will be no marriage there as we understand the concept.

How does this encounter relate to any situation a Christian may face in modern times? Maybe we can equate the Sadducees with the atheists of our own time. No, the Sadducees were not unbelievers in that sense, but with their denial of the resurrection, they might as well have been. Like skeptics of today, they apparently believed that physical death was the end of personal existence.

Sadducees may have thought that by presenting Jesus with an untenable situation in the resurrection they might discredit his own teaching.

The militant atheist or agnostic would seek to do the same by posing such a question as this to a Christian: If you worship an all-powerful and all-loving God, as you say, how is it that he allows starvation, child abuse, wars and natural disasters?

Those on that side of the spiritual equation might imagine they have scored an irrefutable point against the existence of the God of the Bible. In actual fact, the Christian has an answer to such questions, but first we might examine the situation from the atheists' point of view.

In their supposedly godless world, the evils they cited are still here. We still have starvation, abuse, man killing man, and earthquakes. What is the unbelievers' answer to that? We can assume they would merely shrug their shoulders and say "that's just life, the way things are." They would live out their lives hoping for the best outcome, then die as the final escape from whatever pain and unhappiness came their way. A rather bleak outlook.

So why does a loving God permit tragedy and misfortune in the world? Because since the sin in the Garden of Eden, this is a fallen world, one in which people get sick, one in which evil people do evil things, one in which nature itself sometimes convulses, but also it is one in which man has the free will to choose good over evil. No, this is not yet paradise, but the good news is that a paradise is in store for those who will accept the gospel truth.

Unlike the hopeless prospect of the atheist, the Christian can look to the certainty of redemption, the plan and work of the all-powerful, all-loving God the unbelievers mock.

In effect, the Sadducees of Jesus' time have their spiritual descendents in our own. While the deniers of old used a scenario based on the resurrection of the dead, in which they did not believe, to try to discredit that teaching, the atheists of today cite what they find to be the shortcomings of a god whose very existence they deny.

MINING FOR NUGGETS

The 23rd chapter of Matthew chapter contains what appear to be distinct teachings from which we can learn something of the Christian life and the deeper realities of God's relationship to his people.

(23:1-3) Here Jesus makes what seems an unusual statement regarding the Pharisees and scribes inasmuch as the remaining passage is spent in rather severe castigation of their actions and attitudes.

These Jewish leaders are, he said, occupying the seat of Moses and therefore Jesus's followers should adhere to their teachings but refrain from emulating their lives. Do as they say but not as they do, because "they don't practice what they preach." (Matthew 23-3)

Does this mean that everything the Pharisees taught was correct? Probably not, but perhaps Jesus meant that to the extent they were faithful to the Mosaic code as it was to be observed, their words could be heeded. The statement may reveal a respect Jesus retained for the foundation of the new covenant he was bringing into being.

Paul may have had much the same thing in mind as Jesus in Philippians 1:15-18 when he said that some preach out of envy and self-interest, but no matter, they were still presenting the gospel, and in that he rejoiced..

So what do we draw from these points? Just this. The message is more important than the messenger. We may find that a minister is flawed in some way. That does not necessarily mean we should discount everything he says.

(23:16-22) This passage, written in highly symbolic terms, admittedly could be read in different ways. But at minimum, it speaks to the error of elevating the secondary at the expense of the primary. In addressing the Pharisees, Jesus seems to say they keep their rules and rituals, but lack the spirit of the law in their heart. The first four verses say that if they had the most important thing, the temple and the altar, they also would get the gold and the offering within them. With the true spirit, the rules then would no longer be an issue.

The last two verses of the passage make clear the Lord Jesus was not talking about some abstraction or object to be sought, but a person, none less than he himself, and when we have him we also have God the Father, as the 22nd verse indicates.

An application for our own time could be about those who profess a belief and adherence to the teachings of Jesus, but not to the Lord himself. Such individuals probably would call Jesus a prophet, a teacher, a great and moral man, but would deny his divinity. What they should know is the lesson the Lord taught in this chapter: If they accept him for who he is, they will get the rest, that is his principles and the blessings that go with them.

(Matthew 23:23) Perhaps this verse is a continuation in the same vein as above, but it also teaches that some righteous acts are more important than others. Here, the Lord describes the giving of tithes and offerings as less important than "the more important matters of the law," which are "justice, mercy and faithfulness." It would seem God values the spiritual condition of the heart above the performance of what might be seen as Christian duties.

But what is equally important is that both categories are desired. It is not a case of either/or. Individual Christians and whole denominations may fall into the error of de-emphasis of one side or the other. In the church world we have the evangelicals on one hand and the social gospel advocates on the other, often to the neglect of the opposite virtue, while Jesus admonishes us not to neglect either.

(Matthew 23:30-32) Here is the condemnation of hubris, no matter what the spiritual issue is. In this case it stems from Jesus' accusation that the Pharisees and their fathers were guilty of sin against the prophets. He attributed to those present their insistence they would not have acted in such a way had they lived in the days of their fathers.

Jesus put it back on them, saying "you testify against yourselves" (Matthew 23:31) to the effect that their ancestors were guilty of murdering the prophets. Essentially the warning to us is that we should avoid such pride as to declare we would never commit this or that sinful act, past or present Remember Peter's assurance to Jesus not many hours before he denied him.

This chapter of the Gospel of Matthew, together with so many others, is like entering a gold mine in search of the riches to be found therein. I pray at least some nuggets came to our attention.

DAY OF CRUCIFIXION

A hymn often sung in churches on Easter mornings starts, "Were You There When They Crucified My Lord?" It's a fair question. Maybe a more realistic question is whether we, together with all of humanity, were represented in some way by those who actually were present in Jerusalem on an April day in about AD 30. That's the subject of this study as we examine eight individuals or groups who were party to those events.

We start with Pontius Pilate (Matthew 27:23-24). Pilate is reported as saying he found no guilt in Jesus, and one verse has him washing his hands of any responsibility for the Lord's death. Pilate in that respect represents all who would imagine it is possible to avoid making a decision about Jesus. The washing of hands, though literal, was symbolic of that fact as well. The Roman governor also can be likened to those who actually praise Jesus, calling him a great teacher, a prophet, an outstanding man, but without accepting him as Lord of all. Such are with us today.

(Mark 15:6-13) Next is what we could call the crowd, or perhaps the mob. These were people – we don't know how many – who were observing the trial of Jesus before Pilate. Their preference for Barabbas, a murderer, over the innocent Jesus is consistent with a world view that embraces evil over good, as ours in many ways has done. That crowd urging crucifixion was one caught up in what was popular in the moment, following the lead of the supposedly smart people of their culture, the opinion-shapers in the world, just as much of the public does in our own time.

When Jesus prayed to the Father, "Forgive them, for they do not know what they are doing," (Luke 23-24) he surely had this mob in mind, because they had no idea this was the Son of God they would see go to the cross. Jesus' words are not blanket absolution but they surely mean that forgiveness, and therefore salvation, was open to even those people and others participating in the crucifixion.

Next comes Thief No. 1, the criminal on a cross to Jesus' left (Luke 23:39). To whom would we liken him? He represents the unrepentant sinner. He is one who in even acknowledging the possibility of a God, sees him only as a way to serve his immediate personal interest. This thief wants to be off the cross so he can resume his life, presumably in like manner as in his past. He is like the man today who prays to be delivered from a bad circumstance, maybe even promising to do better, but who probably would go back to his sinful ways unchanged by the experience.

Thief No. 2, the one on Jesus' right (Luke 23:40-43), obviously comes to salvation here, as Christians have done through the ages, but his case differs from most. The Christian anthem, "I Came By the Way of the Cross," describes this man as one who brought no virtues, no good works with him. He may have lived his entire life to that point without committing a single decent act and yet found redemption with a simple request. It was the barest statement of faith. First he recognized Jesus' innocence, perhaps even his holiness, then he confessed his own guilt, call it sinfulness. Finally this criminal understood he and the righteous man to his left both would die that day but that there is yet a kingdom waiting. "Jesus, remember me when you come into your kingdom," he said (Luke 23: 42), a most modest plea, which the Savior immediately honored.

What turned this man to the Lord? The Bible doesn't tell us, but here's a thought:

When the thief heard that Jesus could offer forgiveness to those who, without just cause, had beaten, stripped, mocked and finally crucified him, maybe that was the moment he knew he was in the presence of deity itself.

And Barabbas? He deserved to die, but the sinless Jesus became his substitute by taking his place. So Barabbas is all of us and we are Barabbas. End of story.

(Matthew 27:41-43) Here we have the chief priests, the top level of the Jewish establishment. They were the mockers, acting in total self-interest under the guise of religious and moral rectitude and exulting in apparent triumph in this drama. In a broad sense, we have their equivalent today in academia, politics, media, business and entertainment. This is the intelligentsia, the wise and beautiful people whose values are propagated and copied in the popular culture.

The Roman soldiers: These were hard men and to them crucifixions were all in a day's work. Typically, if they thought about a deity at all they probably ascribed it to Caesar. But at 3 p.m., as Jesus died and nature itself convulsed in torment, the callousness of at least one, perhaps more, of the soldiers was penetrated. The centurion represents those among us who may seem, from the outside, to be beyond the reach of the gospel. The scriptures indicate his conversion came from witnessing Jesus demeanor on the cross (Mark 15:39), but also from the demonstrated power and majesty of God.

(John 19:38) Joseph of Arimathea: Here is one whose counterparts abound in the Christian world. He was a secret disciple because he feared the Jews. Afraid of what? To be physically attacked? To be ostracized by his peers? To be kicked off the Sanhedrin? And what about us? Are Christians ever reluctant to go public, so to speak? The result might be ridicule, loss of social standing, or possibly detriment to career. As recorded in Mark 15:43, Joseph found his courage in a major way when he went to Pilate to claim the body of Jesus so he could place him in his own tomb. He was declaring to one who had temporal life-and-death authority over him that yes, he was now an open follower of the Lord regardless of consequences.

So we come back to the original question. Were we there? With certainty, we can know our sin was there. We also can say that one way or another we and others around us were represented by those who actually were present in that time and place. And we should consider this question: Had we been on the scene at Calvary, would we have acted any better than those who were?

ABOVE ALL, LOVE

This short chapter, 13 verses in 1 Corinthians 13, is one of the Bible's most familiar, but it nevertheless presents a challenge to a fuller understanding beyond what may be an obvious teaching about the paramount importance of love.

Paul's first three verses contain a list of what appear to be five Christian gifts or acts, and these seem to be arranged in ascending order of value and dedication. They might be summarized as golden-tongue oratory, a high level of education, strong faith, sacrificial monetary giving and finally, even martyrdom.

In each case, Paul essentially wrote that if love did not accompany these apparent virtues in Christian performance, they were effectively worthless. This is a hard teaching when one considers the seemingly impressive abilities and forms of service Paul would dismiss in the absence of love.

It perhaps is not hard to imagine a spellbinding speaker, a PhD or a generous contributor operating with a cold heart or even under the sin of hypocrisy. But what about such matters as a faith that could move mountains, or someone willing to give his own life for his cause? We would not assume that those qualities and actions could possibly be devoid of a loving heart. But Paul may be making a point that love, as he defines it, is so basic to the Christian life that even faith and martyrdom, and perhaps those only hypothetically, could exist without the softening quality of love.

It's important to try to understand exactly what kind of love Paul refers to. After all, we know there are at least three biblical definitions of the word from the Greek: Eros, meaning romantic love, philos, meaning brotherly love, and agape, sacrificial love that describes what God bestows on his children and is the highest level embraced by humanity.

Paul devotes four verses in the chapter, 4-7, to describe for us what this kind of love looks like. Mostly the scripture tells of personal qualities, such as patience, kindness, humility, a willingness to forgive, having an even temper and so forth. Of course, these traits also could merely describe a nice person regardless of religious conviction, so Paul must have had more in mind. And as he continued down his list of virtues, he seemed to reach for a deeper meaning of love, such as steadfastness in trust plus a clear recognition and godly reaction to truth versus evil.

Thus we conclude that Paul's definition of love is not a superficial veneer of pleasantness but the very essence of Christian demeanor that overlays what Jesus called the greatest commandments, which is to love God and to love your neighbor as yourself.

That leaves us with the thought that what Paul described in the opening verses as ability and service devoid of love was about those whose very inner being of heart and soul stunted the talents they possessed, even to the point of canceling them out. Conversely, had the love Paul described been present, it might have given spiritual life to great preaching, impressive education, generous stewardship and the rest.

It is possible that during his ministry Paul became aware of such men, those who seemed to have every tool to be a great servant of God, but were harsh in judgment, impatient with less than perfection, quick tempered, unforgiving. Even though Paul used unyielding language in calling the work of such individuals as essentially worthless, it is doubtful he would have written off an actual person so readily. Redemption is always a possibility in New Testament teaching.

At verse 8, Paul seems to shift his emphasis by declaring that while love will last, other aspects of the spiritual life will not. These include prophecy, knowledge and charismatic worship. His acknowledgement of incomplete understanding emphasizes the one thing he is certain of: the lasting nature of love that infiltrates the spirit.

As the chapter winds down, the apostle shifts from his incomplete human knowledge to the prospect of full heavenly disclosure marked most particularly by seeing the Lord as he is and by reciprocal recognition, knowing that Jesus will see him as he had become. From Paul's standpoint, it is a glorious conclusion to the discussion.

In his benediction of the chapter Paul named the three spiritual essentials: faith, hope and love. And it is the last of those that is first in rank, because, perhaps, he knew the other two also would be contained therein.

There is a postscript to this chapter from the secular world. In the 1950s, crooner Don Cornell presented a popular song with the title of Paul's three essential virtues. It's interesting that there was a time in our society when the popular music business could produce a work that so eloquently reflected a biblical truth. One line in the song goes, "How do I know, the Bible tells me so."

And so it does.

KEEPING THE FAITH

The epistle to the Galatians by the Apostle Paul is heavy in theology and also offers some personal insights about the man. The main theme and possibly the real reason he wrote the letter at all was a falling away from the true gospel by some of the newly converted Galatian Christians.

Paul's disappointment is apparent in the sixth verse of the first chapter. He expressed dismay and surprise that the people's spiritual lapse had happened so quickly.

Paul in describing the problem is not overly specific but from his language we can deduce that these are Jewish proselytes who have come under devious influence to turn back toward their former ways, such as observing beliefs and traditions of Judaism that faith in Jesus had displaced.

It apparently was this failing that led Paul into a detailed discussion of the law and grace, which might be summed up in its simplest terms with one verse essentially stating that had the law been able to save, Christ's death would have been unnecessary (2:21).

Along the way the apostle detoured into a biographical disclosure about his life before conversion and his activities in the early aftermath. Verses 13-14 of Chapter 1 might be particularly revealing about the zeal with which Paul persecuted Christians when he was known as Saul.

His statement, perhaps even a boast, that he was outperforming many other men of his own age and was advancing in the ranks of Judaism may tell us that religious fervor was not his only motivation. Perhaps he also was driven by personal ambition, a desire for upward mobility, and found defense of the established Jewish beliefs as the vehicle.

This reading of scriptural meaning in no way disparages Paul's character as a Christian, because this was the man before, not after, his Damascus road encounter with Christ.

After that, according to his narrative, Paul purposely waited three years before going to Jerusalem, the heart of both Judaism and Christianity. Instead, he spent that time in Arabia, apparently trying to absorb his conversion experience. He was clear about one thing: The truth of the Christian faith did not come from instruction by any man, but rather as revelation from Jesus Christ (1:12).

That assertion is pertinent in a secondary way, if the authorship of the book of Hebrews is an issue, as it is with some. In that epistle, the writer mentions that a Christian teaching from the Lord was related to him by those who were present, indicating that the writer was not present. Paul's statement that he did not learn an important truth from another man could be taken to suggest he did not write Hebrews.

Eventually Paul did travel to Jerusalem where he met Peter and James, but no other apostles. So the point may be that despite the dramatic aspects of his conversion, Paul went about his apostolic development with care and deliberation, which probably served him well.

Paul's reliance on revelation and not man seems to indicate that Christian faith is not learned second-hand but must be personal. This is consistent with the gospel account of Peter's great confession that Jesus was the Son of God. Jesus declared that the revelation did not come by man but by God the Father (Matthew 16:17).

Regarding Peter, Paul told the Galatians about the confrontation he had had with his fellow apostle at Antioch when Peter, who customarily ate with the Gentile Christians, refused to do so when visiting Jews were present (Galatians 2:11-14). We can easily relate that incident to any Christian who behaves one way with his church friends and another with perhaps the old crowd he once ran with. It is not an uncommon failing, especially among fresh converts.

Paul may have believed the experience with Peter at Antioch was pertinent to the problem at hand in Galatia where some Christians apparently had reverted to their former Jewish beliefs and rituals. Peter's snubbing of the Gentiles in favor of his Jewish friends could have been seen by the Galatians as akin to their own situation and the seriousness with which Paul viewed it. After all, the apostle was willing to rebuke a man he loved and respected to his face in front of other people. That gave the Galatians some indication how strongly Paul felt about their own error.

Paul spends most of the latter chapters of the book in deep theological discussion about grace and the law, hoping to restore the Galatians to the liberty they enjoyed in Christ rather than the burden of the law, which they could not keep.

While the analogy might not be perfect, the Galatians' fault in returning to their former ways and beliefs is not much different from what Christians today might experience when tempted to return in some respect to the sinful life they once knew. The Galatians needed restoration, and other Christians through the ages have often required the same.

FAMILIES, EARTH AND HEAVEN

Chapters five and six of Paul's epistle to the Ephesians deal, in part, with three main issues: earthly families, Christ's relationship with his church, and the importance of lines of authority. All are intertwined between Ephesians 5:22-29 and 6:1-9.

Paul starts with marriage, essentially instructing wives to be subject to their husbands and the men to love their wives. That passage has fallen victim to both controversy and misunderstanding. It needn't have. First, its meaning is sufficiently clear and second, its principle is completely consistent with the overall message of the Bible.

The misconception stems from a shallow reading of 5:22, which was taken by some to mean that women must suffer under total domination by their husbands regardless of the treatment they receive. That in turn has led to the controversy, evident by some of the outside reaction to one denomination's emphasis on the passage.

So we need to look at the scripture more closely. Note the phrase, "as to the Lord," (Ephesians 5:22) in the instruction to the wives on submission. And when Paul got to the husbands, he ended his injunction with this phrase: "just as Christ loved the church and gave himself up for it." (Ephesians 5:25)

Viewed in that light, a man in such a marriage would not be a bully or an unyielding boss and the wife would not be intimidated into not having a will of her own. It would not mean the husband would get his way on every point. To the contrary, sacrificial love might often mean the husband yielding to the wife's desires and best interest. Her submission most properly would be to her husband's spiritual leadership, should he exercise it as he should.

In this arrangement, it can truthfully be said that the female partner receives the better part of it. How do we know this? Because Paul made clear in this passage the direct comparison between earthly marriage and the Lord's relationship to his church. And in that sense, it is certain that the Lord made the sacrifice and the church, the bride of Christ, has reaped the benefit through salvation and the blessings of Christian life. The spousal analogy thus is consistent.

This connection between Christ's relation with his church and an earthly marriage was a masterstroke of teaching by Paul, because he taught truths about each from the comparison with the other, thus increasing his readers' understanding of both: The spiritual truth and the earthly relationship. The eternal and the temporal.

He taught that Christ is head of the church just as the husband is head of the wife. That latter statement still may give feminists heartburn, but we must consider again the two sides of each relationship. They center on two words: Submission and sacrifice. As Christians, we submit our lives to Christ, and his sacrificial death gives us eternal life. On earth, the wife submits to a husband who would, if necessary, give his life for her, and in a more ordinary way is prepared to give up much for a loving wife.

Paul expanded his teaching about family by bringing children into the picture, admonishing them to obey their parents and then instructing the adults to deal with sons and daughters with fairness, kindness and patience, and most particularly to "bring them up in the training and instruction of the Lord." (Ephesians 6:4)

What's important is that all figures in a family -- father, mother, children -- have a responsibility and also receive benefits from the others as a result.

Paul had already made the point that there is a line of authority in God's economy, starting with Christ, then to the husband as head of the household. But also, he expanded the idea in Ephesians 6 to include the mutual responsibility between slave and master, or we might say employee and boss, requiring willing obedience and loyalty by the former and consideration and fairness by the latter. His point is that no matter how exalted a person's status is in the world, he is still accountable to a higher authority and has a godly obligation to those of lower estate.

The relationship of Christ to his church, as Paul described it, is an unassailable truth. The analogy to marriage and the family reflects an ideal, not necessarily reality in this imperfect life. We would have to admit that most families do not always live up to that ideal, but we can strive to follow those general principles. The extent to which families succeed in this surely pleases God.

PRIMITIVE LIGHT

Paul, on his way to Rome in order to carry out his appeal to the emperor, had endured a long and hazardous sea voyage, which ended in shipwreck on the island of Malta (Acts 28:1-10). All aboard made it safely ashore. There can be no doubt that Paul's trip to Rome, though ostensibly the outcome of his trial in Judea, was part of God's plan for his life and ministry.

Paul and the others were greeted in a friendly way by the Maltese, and a fire was built to ward off the chill. A venomous snake came out of the fire and bit Paul on the hand, which caused the natives to conclude that he must be a murderer, and a fatal snakebite was his just punishment by the god(s) they recognized.

The question arises: Where did these primitive island people living far from the center of Christian-Judeo teaching get such ideas, that first, murder is wrong and second, that divine judgment of it is in order?

Paul himself may have provided an answer in three verses in Romans (1:18-20). Though he approached the subject negatively, discussing the decline of man into depravity, the teaching can be positive also. By that passage, the apostle begins to address an issue that has concerned Christians for many years, and that is how people who have never had the chance to hear the gospel can be held responsible and also to find salvation.

Paul seems to tell us that anyone simply by observing the natural creation can know something of God. Beyond that, this person might discern that such a being must be good, and further that man is accountable to Him. Thus we might believe that once the first limited light is responded to, more light is given. And finally, Paul declares that there is no excuse for failing in that response.

So we come back to the Maltese. They were kind, and they knew that murder and apparently other transgressions violated a natural order and would be judged. Of course, they were not fully enlightened because once Paul survived the snakebite, they reversed themselves and thought Paul to be a god himself until he disabused them of that idea.

But here's the payoff. Paul spent three more days among the Maltese, healing people, and, we can be sure, sharing the gospel of Christ among those ready to hear it. His message was an addition to the light they already had received from nature, and we can believe that receiving the full truth was their reward for that.

The breaking up of a ship at that particular island surely was no random event, but was a divine appointment of God to put the Apostle Paul together with a particular people at a given time. We can suppose that our own apparent chance encounters in life may be divinely arranged as well.

UNWORTHY COMPARISONS

Scripture can be found that in effect reminds Christians their behavior might suffer in comparison to that of some unbelievers. It's a cautionary teaching.

Two such passages come to mind, one a single verse in the New Testament, the other a whole chapter in the Old Testament.

1 Timothy 5:8 states that an individual who does not take care of his own "has denied the faith and is worse than an unbeliever." That seems to be a straightforward statement needing no interpretation.

But worse than an unbeliever? Spiritually speaking, who can be worse than someone who in one way or another has rejected Christ and his offer of salvation? And if the uncaring one Paul describes is worse than an unbeliever, it follows that the person must be a Christian oneself. It is a stinging indictment of one who by definition is part of the body of Christ.

To be sure, this teaching is not confined to relative work ethic, but has many other applications that might contrast the life of a Christian unfavorably with that of an unbeliever – such matters as honesty, temperament, personal habits and others.

Jeremiah 35 offers another perspective on the subject. Here we see representatives of the Recabite tribe invited by the prophet, under direction by God, into a holy place in Jerusalem. Recabites were a nomadic people mentioned in the Old Testament on occasion. In this situation, they had made their home in Judea for their own protection.

Jeremiah, as instructed, simply offered the invitees some wine to drink. The Recabites refused it, citing their tribal rule, as well as other standards by which they were to live.

That scene was about the extent of the exchange between Jeremiah and the Recabites. The prophet then turned his attention to Israelites, and the scriptural discourse essentially took this tone: This pagan tribe demonstrated far greater obedience to its own code of conduct than that shown by the Israelites (God's own people, the descendents of Abraham, children of promise and in the biological pipeline that would lead to the Messiah). Jeremiah reminded them of their idolatry and other specific lapses to prove his point.

Not stated in the scripture but noteworthy nevertheless is that these pagans had been brought into an environment where it could have been less difficult for them to violate their own ethic by drinking the wine. They might have rationalized that they were guests, that they might please their host by doing so, that the rest of the tribe would never know and so forth. How many times have Christians found themselves in a comparable situation and not acted as faithfully as the Recabites did?

So the message is clear. Sometimes God's people, whether the Israelites of old or Christians of today, can come off poorly when measured against the lives of those outside the fold of faith.

In our own time, we might make this comparison to a communistic atheist, a true believer in Marxism. In the marketplace of ideologies, would the typical Christian speak out as boldly in defense of his faith as a dedicated Communist or militant atheist would in declaring his own conviction? Or could someone conclude, as Jeremiah did to the Israelites, that the Christian's adherence to his beliefs at times did not measure up to that of the secular world?

The story was once told of a confirmed infidel chiding a Christian with something like this: "If I believed what you say you believe, I would crawl on my hands and knees over broken glass to get that message to others." An excessive boast perhaps, but it makes its point.

We must hasten to declare that the scenarios offered above are not the norm, but the exceptions, at least in the church age. Christian people by and large do live upright lives, conspicuously true to their faith, by comparison to the ungodly world around them. But as the scriptures remind us, we must take care that our walk with the Lord does not leave room for the accusation that we Christians do not behave any better, or perhaps even worse, than those who profess no faith at all.

CHOSEN FOR DESTINY

What did the Pharaoh of Egypt, Haman of Persia, Herod of Judea, the Fuhrer of Germany and now the Ayatollahs of Iran have in common? The first four practiced a form of genocide against the Jews and the last seek to do so.

One inescapable conclusion we can draw from these historical and present facts is that there must be something quite special about a race of people who arose in what we now call the Middle East or Holy Land early in recorded human history.

Of course, even a cursory examination of the Bible tells us much on the subject, primarily that the Israelites, the descendants of Abraham, Isaac and Jacob, were chosen by God as his people.

The wit Ogden Nash once observed, " How odd of God to choose the Jews."

So the questions arise: Why was there a need for a chosen people? One answer (though surely not the only one) might be that the chosen served as the entryway for God's direct involvement with the human race, meaning that through this one selected people he would reveal himself, establish a relationship, set forth standards through the law, exercise judgments, and promulgate a plan to bring his creation into lasting fellowship with him.

God promised Abraham and later Jacob that they would be a blessing to all nations. Whatever else that declaration might mean, we can be certain its main fulfillment would be the coming of the Christ as Savior from our penalty for sin. The incarnate Son of God would be born from a direct line through Abraham and certain descendents.

That God would accomplish this through a single race rather than through a disparate and scattered mankind makes sense even from human logic. But why the Jews? God alone has the answer to that, but considering the history of the people, it is fair to wonder. The scriptures go to great length detailing the disobedience, stubbornness, idolatry, and rebellion of God's chosen. Yet they survived as a people and are with us today, with an identity and by many measures exceptional.

One does not have to be a reader of the Bible to see that. Is it not remarkable that ethnic Jews, religious or not, are so good at so many things, excelling in commerce, law, finance, entertainment and other fields far beyond their numbers. American lore is rife with Jewish families arriving on these shores with nothing, starting a humble work, and ending in wealth and prominence. Others have done the same, but it seems that Jewish people have been particularly successful.

Remember the Six-Day war of 1967? Little Israel was surrounded by Arab enemies bent on its destruction. The outcome speaks for itself. And Hitler thought Jews were too soft to fight.

Let's revisit the genocide history. After Jacob led his small party of 70 souls to Egypt to join his son Joseph and avoid starvation (Genesis 46:26-27), the Jews multiplied to the point that Pharaoh became alarmed. He took the long view, deciding that if he did not allow any male Israelite newborns to survive, eventually the race would decline and die off entirely (Exodus 1:22). Moses, of course, was spared by divine intervention for the great work he would do for the people.

The evil Haman had a different motivation for killing all the Jews. Mostly it was hatred and jealousy of the Jew Mordecai, cousin of Queen Esther, and also as a way to curry favor with the king, who had made Haman his prime minister. His plan backfired; the Jews in the kingdom fought back against those who would do them harm and Haman was hanged on the gallows he had built for Mordecai (Esther 7:10).

Herod's problem was fear that the birth of one considered to be the Jewish messiah would become a threat to his position and authority. So he ordered the death of every male born in Judea over the previous two years just to be sure that the infant Jesus would be included (Matthew 2:16). God's intervention through a dream to Joseph thwarted that evil scheme.

The closest anyone came to total annihilation was Adolph Hitler, who saw the elimination of the Jewish race as the "final solution." His motivation may have been a combination of racial hatred, a design to preserve what he considered the superior Aryan race and scapegoating to induce the Germans to galvanize behind their blame of Jews for all their troubles.

The current state of Iran is on record in its desire to eradicate the Jewish state of Israel. How that will develop is yet to be seen.

Even apart from the genocide attempts there has been a long history of anti-Semitism that persists to a degree in Europe and the United States to this day. Thus we have continued evidence of Jewish exceptionalism that can have no other effect than confirmation of biblical truths.

There will be no attempt here to discuss the so-called replacement theology that seeks to define the Christian body of Christ as a substitute for the biblical Israel. Nor will British Israelism be considered. That belief concerns the 10 lost tribes of Israel, the northernmost that were taken into captivity and then essentially disappeared. British Israelism holds that those tribes settled Europe and many migrated to the new world, thereby establishing western civilization.

Don Gordon

What we can believe with some conviction is that Jews still matter, that the state of Israel matters, and that God is not finished with his people chosen by him perhaps 40 centuries ago. How this all will play out will be revealed in the fullness of time

Printed in the United States
by Baker & Taylor Publisher Services